# WORTH THE CLIMB

## *A BLACK AMERICAN WOMAN'S PURSUIT OF CORPORATE SUCCESS*

AUDREY J. SNYDER, MS

## DEDICATION

To all who think they are alone in the struggle. Be encouraged: others have cried, suffered, and endured so you can succeed. Never allow obstacles or anger to block your path to success.

# WORTH THE CLIMB

## *A BLACK AMERICAN WOMAN'S PURSUIT OF CORPORATE SUCCESS*

Audrey J. Snyder, MS

*This book was written and published in partnership with inCredible Messages, LP*
*www.inCredibleMessages.com*

WORTH THE CLIMB
Copyright © 2012 by Audrey J. Snyder, MS

To contact the author, Audrey Snyder, visit
WorthTheClimb@yahoo.com

To contact the publisher, inCredible Messages Press, visit
www.inCredibleMessages.com

Printed in the United States of America

ISBN 978-0-9847983-7-7      Paperback
ISBN 978-0-9847983-8-4      e-Book
- Autobiographical
- Black American
- Cultural Heritage

Book Coaching and Editing:  Bonnie Budzowski, inCredible Messages, LP

Cover Design:  Gwen Loughner, Wordcrafters

Interior Design:  inCredible Messages, LP

Author Photo:  Benton Design Photography

Published by inCredible Messages Press

To protect confidentiality, names, locations, and some details of the stories in this book have been changed.

# ACKNOWLEDGEMENTS

Thanks to my Lord and Savior who guided my thoughts and hands through the writing of each chapter of this book. To HIM I am eternally grateful.

Much respect and honor to my great-great grandmother Ringgold who set the example that I must pursue my dreams.

Much appreciation and love to Auntie Frances whose youthful attitude and spirit at the age of 95 inspire me to keep pursuing excellence.

Thanks to my husband, Nate, who gave me patience and priceless love throughout the writing of this book. I thank God for you.

Thanks to my children, Nate Jr. and Michele, who didn't complain during the endless hours I spent building my career.

To Beverly Jones, thank you for your honest truths and prayers throughout my struggles to write about reality.

Heartfelt appreciation to my friend, Bill Travis Jr., for believing in me and being there always with encouragement and support when I doubted myself.

Thanks to Bonnie Budzowski of inCredible Messages who helped me get in touch with my inner feelings which detail the essence of this book.

Thanks to all my family and friends who encouraged me and prayed for my success.

# Author's Notes

## Names and Locations

In sharing my personal pursuit of corporate success, I've chosen to change the names of the companies, locations, and many of the people in the story. This is because my goal in writing is to share my own struggles and what I've learned through them, rather than to point angry fingers. If I've learned one thing about success as a person, it's that dwelling in anger won't get you there.

## The Term, Black American

While writing this book, I struggled with the terms Negro, African American, and Black American. The label was important to me because society makes perceptions based on ethnic classifications.

Merriam-Webster Dictionary defines African American as "an American of African and especially of Black African descent." Macmillan Dictionary defines African American as "someone from the US who belongs to a race of people that has dark skin and whose family originally came from Africa."

The Civil Rights Act of 1964 and the Voting Rights Act of 1965 were landmarks in the lives of many blacks in America because it represented a change in consciousness. Personally, I was grateful for the song from James Brown, "Say It Loud—I'm Black and I'm Proud," recorded in 1968. I had graduated from high school three years prior and had completed my associate's degree and was about to enter the corporate world. I was very much aware of my role as a Black American, and Brown's lyrics had an influence on me as well as on society in general. Lyrics have power, and Brown's use of the word "black" rather than "Negro" or "colored" represented a change for many

Americans, especially Black Americans. Brown's song defined a black man as a man who has pride, who wants to make his race mean something. Two sentences from the lyrics of Brown's song struck me. "Brother, we can't quit until we get our share" and "I say we won't quit moving till we get what we deserve." These lyrics caused me to question, am I getting what I deserve? This song was perfect for the changing times of all Black Americans.

The development of Black American culture, which is a combination of African and Western European culture, had created a distinct ethnic group. As I struggled to define my label, the civil rights groups started to define the Black Pride Movement which included terms like *I'm Black and I'm Proud.* As the country went through changes, more radical militant leaders like Malcolm X and Stokely Carmichael advocated the idea of "Black Power." The assertiveness in Brown's lyrics made the song an anthem for the Black Power Movement.

Since my genetic makeup includes Scotch-Irish descent on one side of my family and Cherokee Indian on the other, as well as Black American descent, it didn't seem right that I choose the label African American. Since I practice Western European Culture and not African Culture, I decided my label would be Black American and that is the term I decided to use as I wrote this memoir.

# CONTENTS

# INTRODUCTION

It hasn't always been easy to be me, driven by desire and determination. Great Auntie Frances tells me my life has been about tenacity and strength, two characteristics I inherited from my Cherokee great-great grandmother. I'm proud to tell my story as an extension of my ancestors'.

Grandmother Ringgold traveled by wagon from Oklahoma to Pennsylvania, facing pitfalls and challenges along the 1300+ mile trip. She loaded the wagon with orphaned children who had survived the massacre of Cherokee Indians by white men who wanted their land. Grandfather Ringgold had been among those massacred.

Grandmother Ringgold traveled only after the sun had set, hoping not to attract attention. She did not want to be seen as a woman traveling alone in the wilderness. During the days, it was hot for the children, who had to lie very still and quiet under the tarpaulin. There was little food. Grandmother would stop along the way at stores but could not buy much because she didn't have much money.

Grandmother Ringgold was determined to get to Pennsylvania. She had family living there and wanted her children and the orphaned children to grow up in a land of opportunity. This journey, once completed, would give the children a chance to live full lives. She wanted the children to eventually tell their stories as well as pass along the history of their ancestors.

My grandmother and her sister, Great Auntie Frances, raised me because my mother died when I was four years old. My father, who was a Black American, didn't live with us and had no real influence on my life. My maternal grandfather was a Black American as well.

As I was growing up, my grandmother told me many stories about my great-great grandmother Ringgold. It was a remarkable feat for a woman to travel unescorted over 1300 miles in a covered wagon filled with orphaned children. Grandmother Ringgold had a strong will and steadfast character that allowed her to accomplish many things that were unthinkable in her day.

Throughout my childhood, it seems Grandmother and Auntie Frances were always talking about the days when their father (my great grandfather) went to the backyard garden to gather herbs to heal whatever ailed them, which was a custom for the Cherokee. Although I was always glad to hear about the good old days when things were simple, I wondered when Grandmother would move on. It was 1960 and I didn't have to go to the back yard if I had a headache. I just needed to go to the drugstore and get some aspirin.

Along with the backyard thinking came the belief that there were limits on my future. Grandmother wanted me to be a nurse. My mother had graduated from Howard University as a registered nurse. It was good enough for her, so it should be good enough for me.

The sight of blood made me physically ill, so there was no way I was going into any part of the medical field, including nursing. Eventually, after many arguments with Grandmother about a nursing career, she suggested teaching, not realizing all my experiences with teachers were bad. The only Black American teacher I knew wasn't nice to me. In fact, she was so busy flirting with all the boys in the class that the girls hardly got any attention, let alone learned anything. There was no way I was going into teaching. Although I was just in my teenage years, I knew I didn't have to settle for nursing or teaching.

Many nights Grandmother would remind me of my limitations when I was practicing piano. If I made a mistake, she would say, "I wish you were as good as Ronnie." Ronnie was the young white child of the family for which she cleaned house.

If I didn't bring home all A's, Grandmother would remind me that Ronnie was an A student. I was so sick of the name Ronnie; I decided that if I had any children, none of them would be named Ronnie. My grandmother would always say, "If you want to teach school, you have to have good grades." I was so tired of hearing that same line, I would mumble under my breath that there was no way I would ever be a schoolteacher.

Since I decided success wasn't nursing or teaching school, it would have to be something in the business world. I decided to look for corporate success. I didn't have any role models to use as examples, just the television and newspaper. All the heads of companies appeared to be successful. They had nice homes, shiny new cars, and children who wore name brand clothes. That looked like success to me, and as a young person just graduating from high school; I thought that's what I wanted. I wanted corporate success.

After graduating from high school with honors, I told my grandmother I wanted corporate success, and she said I was silly. She said, "That's *their* (the white people's) world," and pointing to a textbook, she said, "and this is *ours*." We got into a huge argument, and I told Grandmother I couldn't live by her rules. She said, "If you can't live by my rules, then you can't live in my house."

I said, "I'll move because I have to move toward success."

Moving out of my grandmother's house, I found a secure building to move into and started my journey. Leaving my grandmother's house was exciting but also a little scary. I didn't know what would be around the corner for me.

At this same time, I began to record my story in a diary so my mother, whom I hadn't gotten to know, would be proud of me. A diary was a good way for my mother to know of my trials and tribulations along my journey to corporate success. I wanted her to know that I was making choices, the right choices that would affect my future. I wanted her to know I was taking responsibility for my own destiny. I decided that when I joined my mother in heaven, she would read the diary and get to know what I had accomplished.

Writing to my mother was a great comfort, but it also made me question if I needed a bigger audience, if others should know of my desire to achieve, my drive to be the best, my desire to be successful.

Little did I know that in many ways my journey would be as long and arduous as Grandmother Ringgold's 1300+ mile trip in a covered wagon. Often I felt alone, discouraged and ready to give up. But just like Grandmother Ringgold, I had a generation behind me and a generation in front of me depending upon my success. Thank goodness I inherited Grandmother Ringgold's tenacity and strength as well as her drive.

Great, Great Grandmother
Mirah Ringgold

Grandmother
Pearl M. Howze

Auntie
Frances H. Anderson

Mother
Dorothy J. Bigelow

Son
Nathaniel A. Snyder, Jr.

Daughter
Michele D. Snyder

40 Years of Marriage
Nathaniel A. and Audrey J. Snyder

*I've waited my whole life for my opportunity, and now it comes with a bitter taste. I want nothing more than to succeed in corporate life, yet my first opportunity comes, not because my hard work and good performance has been noticed, but because of affirmative action. Should I cling to anger and stand on principle, or should I seize the opportunity and prove to them all that Black Americans can make it in their world?*

CHAPTER 1                                          1976

## BEGINNING MY JOURNEY

As I shut my eyes, I can almost see the day my journey for success began in earnest. It is 1976, 6:00 a.m., a beautiful spring morning. I awake to the chirping of birds and the whisper of trees swaying in the morning breeze. I get up slowly to sit on my window seat and watch the birds sitting in our tree just outside my window. I like to sit and relax for a few minutes before the worries of the day seep in.

My husband, Nate, is supportive of my desire to succeed in the corporate world. Nate believes success comes from hard work and good character. We both meet the criteria and are willing to work hard to be successful.

Nate isn't interested in corporate success for himself; he's more concerned with a successful marriage and family. Because his father left his mother with ten children, Nate is determined to be a true presence and support to our family. Our daughter, Michelle, is now four years old and Nate Jr. is a baby.

It looks calm and peaceful outside, but inside me things are different. I wonder what worries today will bring. Will today be the day I get my chance for success? I am emotionally charged because it is the first day of my new job as a personnel interviewer in the white corporate world.

As dawn is breaking, the world's silence seems to blanket the houses on my block. Even though I'm in a large city, Wesleyville, Ohio, I love the small town atmosphere of our neighborhood where everyone is treated like a relative, an aunt, uncle, brother, or sister. We chose to stay in this part of the city because both Nate and I grew up in this small community, and this is where we want to raise our family.

Although Nate and I haven't discussed how I am going to continue to pursue my dream in my new job while raising a family, I think he just automatically assumes he will be playing a larger role in managing the house.

Opening the window to get some fresh air, I can see my entire neighborhood. As I look, I think of how comforting it is to know that the same families have lived in this neighborhood for years. Their children have grown and the houses have weathered, but the neighborhood seems the same. Now our children will experience the culture of this neighborhood.

Most of the two-story houses have yards in which the children can play. The community playground with swings, monkey bars, and a sliding board is at the end of the well-maintained block. There is even a small basketball court. Sitting on my window seat, looking up and down the block, I see and feel a world where life seems safe, a place where I know everyone and everyone knows me.

Oh, there goes Mr. Tunie. Everyone just calls him Tunie. Tunie lives across the street in the red brick house and is always up early sweeping his walk. He is the neighborhood handy man even though he works during the day as a mechanic for a local garage. You can find Tunie at any house on our block fixing a roof, laying tile, or fixing a clogged sink in his spare time. I can almost hear the neighbors calling him. "Hey Tunie, my car is stalled. Tunie, my sink is clogged. Tunie, can you drive me to the grocery store?"

The best part of living in my neighborhood is the families. Mrs. Chambers mothers all the children, watching everyone from her front porch swing, waving her finger, telling the children to stop throwing stones or candy wrappers on her walk. I'm sure she will take Michelle and Nate Jr. under her wing and make sure they know the rules of the neighborhood when they are old enough. Mrs. Chambers is a widow who spends most of her days baking. I can smell the homemade bread or pies as soon as I get near her house.

Mrs. Chambers spent most of her adult years as a domestic worker who performed work known as day work: cleaning homes, washing clothes, and cooking meals for white families. It was hard work and usually paid below minimum wage. After Mr. Chambers died, she quit cleaning for white folks and stayed around the neighborhood most days watching over us. Mr. Chambers had an insurance policy and a small pension that allows Mrs. Chambers a little comfort to stay at home.

When a new neighbor moves onto our block, Mrs. Chambers makes a welcome basket filled with tea bags and fresh baked pies. She marches right up to the front door and knocks until someone answers. Mrs. Chambers will go into a house and not come out for hours. I'm not sure what they talk about, but when Mrs. Chambers comes out both she and the new neighbor are laughing and hugging each other. Once Mrs. Chambers makes her visit, everyone on my block also welcomes the new neighbor.

It's spring and I can't wait for summer. Summer block parties are the best. Mrs. Chambers organizes the party, getting a permit to block off the street and making sure everyone brings something. There are honey barbecued ribs, fried chicken, corn on the cob, candied yams, collard greens, and all the pies and cakes you can eat. Teddy, our local disc jockey, plays all the latest Motown hits so we can dance until the wee hours of the morning.

At the last block party, Smokey Robinson's "Ooh Baby Baby" played in the background. Someone shouted, "How about a little Stevie Wonder's 'Fingertips'?" Someone else shouted, "How about Martha Reeves and the Vandella's 'Heat Wave'? It sure is hot out here." Teddy tried to keep up with all the requests. People from other neighborhoods came out too, bringing food with them.

Our block parties are popular and word of good times spreads all through town. The parties go on for hours. The streetlights provide the right atmosphere when darkness sets in. Couples pair up when Teddy plays Mary Wells' "Two Lovers," and Marvin Gaye's, "Let's Get It On." Enjoying the music at the last block party, I didn't realize then how much I would someday miss these times and Mrs. Chambers.

Gazing out my window, I wonder if things will ever change. It's 1976, a time when the world is fighting discrimination and quota systems, and at the same time the nation is celebrating the 200th anniversary of the Declaration of Independence. I wonder who the writers of that document thought should be included in the celebration.

Are we all free? Will we ever be free? I still have to prove that I can fit in because Corporate America is still unsure where blacks belong. The Viking spaceship can land on Mars, but Corporate America has not moved past 1950. I still have to show what kind of Black American I am because I don't fit the stereotype of a gun-toting, drug-selling ghetto-dweller.

Having graduated in the top half of my high school class with honors and achieving my Associate's Degree in Secretarial Science, I'm finally on my road to success.

For the last three years, I have worked as a secretary in the Human Resources Department at Tri-State, a large insurance firm that includes a credit union office. The company has several satellite offices in the county. The Human Resource Department is responsible for filling clerical openings in the headquarters, satellite, and credit union offices.

Recently, out of the blue, a department manager, Ms. Schurr, came to my desk and asked if I would like to be considered for a position as a personnel interviewer. I still can't believe it.

For a minute, my heart seemed to stop. All these questions went through my head: Do I want this? Should I? Could I? Do I dare? What if?

Ecstatic though scared, I said, "Yes." I spoke to Ms. Schurr in Standard English, as always. I'm aware that members of Corporate America use black dialect as a code to judge people's intelligence, so I learned to be careful to speak Standard English when I am in their world.

Alone on my window seat, I think, "Wow, I finally made it." Then reality sets in—like a light bulb going off inside my head. It's 1976 and I realize why I am being offered this position. I have seen the reports that come to my department regarding Equal Employment Opportunity Commission (EEOC) commitments, and I know we haven't fulfilled the quota for hiring minorities for the year. Even though I have only been in the department for three months, I fit the need. I am a woman and a minority—two points for the company.

Though the reason behind my promotion has a bitter taste, I decide I don't care that I am being offered the position just to fill a quota or that I will be the token minority. This is my chance, and I am not going to pass it up because I am one of the lucky ones. I am in the right spot at the right time.

At such a juncture, I can't help but think of my grandmother. What would she tell me to do? Would she think I am making a mistake? Would she think the risk is too great? I know Grandmother's definition of success was for me to be a nurse or schoolteacher, but that goes totally against my own point of view. My definition of success lies in the corporate world, their world. This is my time. I am willing to take the risk.

It is 1976 and anti-discrimination laws are being put to the test. I want a little of what Mary McLeod Bethune and Rosa Parks fought for. In 1935, Ms. Bethune founded the National Council of Negro

Women to open new doors for young women with goals and aspirations of becoming successful. I can't let those doors close. Twenty years later in 1955, Rosa Parks' quiet strength launched a boycott of the Montgomery buses for 381 days. Rosa Parks' action changed the lives of many. I want to be part of that change. I know I have to prepare for my future. I owe those who fought before me that much.

It's getting late and I have to get ready for work. Moving from my spot on my window seat, I pay particular attention to my appearance, wanting to make the right impression. Being the only Black American in the department will make me very visible. Looking carefully over my selection of clothes, I choose my two-piece navy blue suit with a white blouse that ties in a bow at the neckline. I pull my polished and shined one-inch navy heels from their box. I can almost see my reflection in these shoes.

I quickly put on my clothes and take a look in my mirror, liking what I see. I am careful about what I eat and have maintained a small waistline even after giving birth. I am 5'-4" and about 105 pounds. I turn around in the mirror a few times. The reflection looking back is that of a professional. My makeup is light, just a little blush on my cheeks and a little lipstick to accent my medium brown complexion. I run my comb over my jet-black hair, styled in the corporate pageboy. This is the latest style that most female professionals, both black and white, are wearing. I choose a gold pin with a pearl inset and small pearl nugget earrings trimmed in gold.

I look at myself one more time in my full-length mirror. I hope both Rosa Parks and Mary Bethune would be proud of my efforts. "I am ready," I think to myself, "ready for whatever lies ahead." I need to prove that I am the right person for this job. Today will be my first test.

I wake Nate up before I leave to get his approval. He tells me how nice I look. I leave the house feeling confident that I am the right person for this job.

It doesn't take long for my first obstacles to surface: peers who do not accept me right away. After all, it was just a few weeks ago that I was their secretary. Now I am doing the same job as they are, with an increase in pay, and I don't have a four-year degree. I have a high school diploma and a two-year associate's secretarial degree. My coworkers are not willing to see me as anything other than a secretary.

As I walk past their offices, I can hear my coworkers scheming and planning about how they aren't going to help me. I hear Sylvia saying, "She thinks she is so smart, let's see what she can do by herself." Lois, another interviewer, tells everyone that as soon as the company meets their quota for hiring minorities, I will be gone. I overhear them talking about how I walk as if I know it all, how I dress like a professional and probably can't afford the clothes I am wearing. They even use some slang terms commonly used in the black neighborhoods, perhaps hoping I will feel embarrassed or ashamed. My coworkers are forming a tight alliance among themselves to make sure they aren't responsible for my success. Every roadblock they put in front of me makes me more determined to succeed.

Most days, as evening approaches, I sit on my window seat, gazing at the happiness right outside my window and wondering how I can leave this calm environment and go back to that office, that abuse. I watch the children playing double-dutch jump rope. Some are drawing lines on the cement for the championship hopscotch matches. Young boys line up for the basketball playoff matches. The children are so innocent. They have no idea what will be in store for them in a few years when it's their turn to enter the corporate world.

Some evenings, I call my girlfriends and talk about how I feel. They say the same thing every time. "Girl, you know you don't have to put up with that crap. Just go down to the EEOC and sue them. That will teach them."

I know legal complaints won't solve anything. In fact, such action would probably make things worse because then everyone in the company would definitely see me as the enemy. I am frustrated that I bothered to call because I knew what my girlfriends would say before they said it. My best course of action is to get a good night's sleep, knowing what to expect in the morning.

Each night, Nate says the same thing, "Tomorrow's another day, another opportunity." That's the last thing I hear each night before I drift off to sleep. In the midst of chaos, Nate and the children are a little bit of heaven.

*The whole point of being alive is to evolve into the complete person you were intended to be.*

*Oprah Winfrey*

*"Whore!" That's what I hear on the other end of the telephone. Years later my ears still ring from Gene Krause's response.*

*Mr. Krause is Corporate America, defined by the media as the ultimate in morality and professional standing in the community. He has ash blonde hair, blue eyes, and the whitest capped teeth ever, adorned in the uniformed three piece navy pinstriped suit, crisp white shirt, dark navy tie, and black wing-tipped shoes.*

*How did it happen that the epitome of Corporate America is on the other end of the phone, blatantly referring to all Black American women as whores? And how am I, a Black American woman charged with sending employment candidates to Mr. Krause, supposed to respond?*

# FACING CHALLENGES

After my initial surge of surprise, fear, and determination at my promotion to recruiter, I settled into my new job and its routine. Arriving at work each day, I passed my peers in the small hallway on the way to my office, saying good morning to everyone whether they returned the greeting or not. Most times, I got no response.

I wondered how long I would be ignored and ostracized. Colleagues should be able to rely on one another, trust each other, and work in harmony. I hoped my peers would see that allies were stronger together than enemies were apart.

After finishing my afternoon appointments, I always offered to help the other interviewers sort applications or arrange appointments. No one took me up on my offer. If fact, no one even answered me. I smiled and kept trying to do the best job I could. I wasn't going to let them win. I was determined they weren't going to break me.

At this point in my career, I still cared about what white people thought of me. I wanted their approval. I wanted to hear them tell me I was doing a good job. I hated to admit it to myself, but I wanted and needed my coworkers' approval and acceptance. I knew the challenge was to stay confident, pick myself up, dust off the embarrassment, put balm on my wounded pride, and move forward.

I felt good about my job and the fact that I was helping others, especially other Black Americans, to get jobs. As the weeks went by, I felt more comfortable at work, but I kept my defenses up.

The company didn't object to hiring Black American applicants as long as they fit the corporate mold. Black Americans had to graduate in the top half of their class in high school to be considered for employment. This wasn't a requirement for other applicants.

The most important qualification for Black Americans, however, was the look. A person's complexion could not be too brown. The company wanted people who were brown enough to be identified as a minority (for the quota system) but not too brown or they might be mistaken for a militant. In addition, a candidate's hair had to be styled in a certain way. Even though the afro hairstyle for Black Americans was popular, any Black American woman who wanted a job in Corporate America had to have straightened hair in the style of the page-boy, a straight blunt cut that fell just below the neck.

Once I screened any candidate, that person's background was checked down to the last detail. Prior work history and references were checked and rechecked before a person could be considered for any position, no matter how entry-level the job. Whenever I had a minority candidate, I didn't leave the reference checking to the secretary; I checked all the references myself. It wasn't that I didn't trust the secretary. I just had to be sure no stone was left unturned.

Federal guidelines were developed on employee selection procedures by the EEOC. These guidelines were developed to aid in the achievement of the nation's goal of equal employment opportunity without discrimination on the grounds of race, color, sex, religion, or national origin. The Federal agencies adopted the guidelines to provide a uniform set of principles governing use of employee selection procedures consistent with generally accepted legal and validation standards.

Tri-State had to stay in compliance with these guidelines. However, their interpretation of the guidelines was slightly altered. Although there was nothing in writing, it was understood by all in the hiring department that it was alright to hire a few minorities to stay in compliance with Federal guidelines for EEOC standards, but no more than absolutely necessary.

One week, I was screening candidates for a job as cashier at the credit union office and, after the process of elimination, I settled on Margaret Ann Fisher as the perfect candidate. I had screened thirty applicants for this position. Margaret met the educational standards and had the related job experience required for the opening.

I called the hiring manager to refer Margaret Ann Fisher, describing her background and experience, telling him she was an excellent minority candidate. There was complete silence on the phone; then the word "whore" was the next thing I heard. The voice on the telephone seemed far away and unreal as it said, "Don't send me any of those black whores you've been referring to everyone else. Black women are nothing but whores and I won't have any of them in my office."

Mr. Krause, the manager, did not realize I was a Black American, one of the black women he was talking about. As my hand began shaking, I held the phone away from my ear, staring at it in disbelief. Finally, I just hung up. Mr. Krause didn't call back, so I'm not sure what he was thinking or if he cared what I was thinking. I didn't have time to worry about Mr. Krause because I was too busy trying to figure out my own feelings. Was my grandmother right? Was this world just for them?

Why did Mr. Krause call Margaret Ann Fisher a "whore"? Margaret Ann wasn't even a typical black name. It sounded more Catholic than Black American. I ran into my coworker Sylvia's office to tell her what had happened. Sylvia seemed a little friendlier than the others. I had felt she was starting to warm up to me. "Sylvia, you won't believe what just happened to me," I blurted out.

"What?" Sylvia replied, still holding the application she was reviewing.

"I was trying to refer an applicant for the opening at the Fifth Avenue Office so I called Mr. Gene Krause, the manager. His exact words were, 'Don't send me any of those black whores you've been referring to everyone.' This is 1977. What happened to affirmative action? What do I do?" I don't think that I even breathed between sentences. I was so upset.

I hadn't stopped to think about using the term black whores to Sylvia or how she would react. I just blurted it out. Sylvia looked up at me with shock on her face. She dropped the application she was reviewing and stared at me. I guess she didn't know what to say. Then after a moment, Sylvia said, "Let's get Ms. Schurr. She will know how to handle this."

We both went down the hall to Ms. Schurr's office. Sylvia knocked on her open door. "Ms. Schurr, do you have a moment; it's important."

"Of course, both of you come in and have a seat."

Sylvia started, "Audrey came to me with a situation I don't know how to handle, so I suggested we come to you." Both Sylvia and Ms. Schurr looked over at me.

Ms. Schurr asked, "Audrey, what happened?" I told Ms. Schurr what happened when I called Mr. Krause about a candidate for referral.

Ms. Schurr looked calmly at Sylvia and said, "Sylvia, please let me talk with Audrey. Thanks for bringing this to my attention."

Ms. Schurr started, "Audrey, I am sorry you had to experience this. I will talk with my manager and see what process we should follow. Are you alright to continue the day or do you need to go home?"

I was shocked. How could she be so calm about this? Why wasn't she outraged at what Mr. Krause said? Why wasn't she more upset?

"No," I said, "I'm alright. I can continue my work. Please let me know what I need to do after you talk with your manager."

Ms. Schurr stood up, giving me the cue to leave. "Everything will be alright, Audrey. Don't worry." How was everything going to be alright? Of course, I would worry.

I passed Sylvia on my way out of Ms. Schurr's office and saw Sylvia and Lois talking in Sylvia's office. They stopped talking when I passed. Sylvia looked up and asked, "Well, what did Ms. Schurr say?"

"She said she would see what the process is," I said, my answer trailing off as I walked down the hall to my office.

Well if Ms. Schurr wasn't going to do anything, I knew what I had to do. I had to meet this man who referred to all Black American women as "whores." I made up my mind to go meet Gene Krause face-to-face.

If I didn't deal with this situation today, how was I going to face tomorrow?

*No one can make you feel inferior without your consent.*

*Eleanor Roosevelt*

*Stunned and angry that a manager can call all Black American women whores without immediate disciplinary action, I know that at the very least I have to look that manager's bigotry in the eye and challenge it. I have to do it for my own sense of self-dignity as well as for the community of Black Americans who will be blocked from success if this man is left unchallenged. But do I have what it takes? How should I handle myself? What should I do or say?*

## OPINION VERSUS REALITY

If I was going to face Gene Krause, I needed courage. A cluster of thoughts flowed through my mind at once. I heard echoes of my own grandmother telling me I would never be as good as white people and shouldn't try to compete in their world. I thought about the stories Auntie Frances told me about Grandmother Ringgold, my ancestor who had the courage to bring all the children from the reservation in Oklahoma to Pennsylvania, facing all kinds of obstacles throughout her journey. I thought about Nate telling me that each day is another opportunity. Deep down, I knew what I had to do. I had to face Gene Krause and show him that all black women weren't whores. I couldn't let my grandmother be right. I had to make Gene Krause see that we could also be a part of his world. I needed to convince him to hire Margaret Ann.

Thinking back, I remembered how excited Margaret Ann was when I called and asked her to come in for the interview. As she walked into my office, she looked elegant, fitting the corporate mold. She was about 5'-8," tall and slender. Her straightened medium-brown hair, styled in the corporate pageboy, accented her fair complexion. She wore a two-piece conservative navy blue suit and a starched white blouse with tapered lapels. The navy blue tailored jacket accented her small waistline. She wore neutral nylons and navy blue heels. Margaret Ann didn't need much makeup because her complexion was flawless. She wore a little blush on her cheeks and a light orange lipstick that gave her fair skin a little color. Her appearance showed she was the perfect candidate for the corporate world.

Margaret Ann and I went through her application carefully, talking about each job she had held in the greatest detail. We focused on her years as a cashier at neighborhood grocery stores and as an inventory clerk. We talked about her family background, growing up in the suburbs with college-educated parents. Margaret Ann hadn't picked up the "ghetto slang" because her parents wouldn't allow it. I had checked and rechecked her references myself, leaving no stone unturned. All her references came back favorable. There was no reason Margaret Ann shouldn't get the job. Yet, Mr. Krause refused to even talk with her because she was a black female.

That's why I had to get up the courage to face him today, for Margaret Ann and for me. I wanted Gene Krause to know his opinion of me could never be my reality.

I walked slowly down the five blocks to Gene Krause's office on Fifth Avenue. It seemed like I had been walking for miles. It was 11:00 a.m., a crisp morning with the sun just beginning to peek over the clouds. I wasn't sure if the little bumps on my arms were from the cool air or from nervousness. As I walked, I rehearsed my entrance in my mind. "Hello, I'm Audrey Snyder from Human Resources. Hello, I'm Audrey Snyder and I'm here to discuss Margaret Ann Fisher's application with you." I rehearsed each opening carefully, wondering which one I should use. I decided I would wait until I saw Mr. Krause. Then I would know exactly what to say and do.

The closer I got to the office, the more nervous I got. When I finally opened the glass door, which seemed to weigh a ton, I looked around to check the atmosphere of the office. On the main floor, there were two customer service clerks on the left side of the floor. Each clerk looked up from his or her desk as I entered the office. On the other side of the floor were four clerks lined up behind a glass partition. Each clerk had his or her own station to serve customers. The first thing I noticed was that no Black American employees were visible to the public. I kept looking around until I heard a deep voice in the background.

"Are you looking for something or are you just checking the place out?" I paused and looked toward the voice. It was a large white man about 6'-2", about 250 pounds, blond with a receding hairline. Dressed in a grey security guard uniform, he was walking toward me from the end of the line of clerks. He had a nightstick on his waist and kept his hand keyed on it. I guess he thought I was there to rob the cashiers.

"Yes," I answered, "I'm looking for Gene Krause."

With a puzzled look, the guard pointed and said, "His office is on the right behind the glass doors."

I looked back and to my right. The little bumps were back. I was really nervous now, but I knew I couldn't show it. From where I was standing, I could see a huge office with a man sitting behind a large desk. Krause's office was furnished in Early American décor, including a light beige couch with large flowers embedded in the fabric. His desk was long and narrow with a glass top. Few furnishings sat on the desk.

As I started towards the office, I heard footsteps behind me. The security guard was hot on my heels. I could hear him breathing behind me and turned and said, "It's alright, Mr. Krause is expecting me."

"Oh," he said after giving me the once over.

As I got close to the doorway, Mr. Krause looked up from his desk and stood up. There he was, the epitome of Corporate America blatantly referring to all black women as whores. Here was Mr. Corporate America, defined by the media as the ultimate in morality and professional standing.

Mr. Krause looked at me with wide eyes. I think he was shocked to see a black woman coming toward him. We both entered his doorway at the same time. I extended my arm to shake his hand and introduce myself.

"Hello," I said, "I'm Audrey Snyder from Human Resources. I spoke to you this morning about an applicant named Margaret Ann Fisher."

I was proud of the way my voice stayed firm and confident. I didn't quiver when I spoke and looked Gene Krause directly in the eye. For his part, Gene Krause stood very silent for a minute, staring and refusing to extend his hand. His only response was a monotone, "Oh."

After a minute of dead silence, I said, "Mr. Krause, I walked from my office because I felt it was necessary for us to meet after your comments this morning. I feel you owe me an apology, and more importantly, I feel you should take a serious look at the applicant I referred for your open position." Offering the application I said, "Margaret Ann Fisher is a minority candidate with all the required qualifications."

Without even looking at me, Mr. Krause snatched the application from my hand and said, "Fine, I'll look at it." He turned around and went back to his desk. I stood there for a full minute watching Mr. Corporate America sit down behind his desk and throw the application in the trash. He swung around in his chair with his back facing me and picked up the phone. He dialed a number and began laughing with someone on the phone.

Well, that was enough for me. I don't know what they were laughing about, but I walked away quickly from his office and out of the building. I knew I had made my point even though Gene Krause didn't seem to care. I knew this was not the end. I would report this incident and let the company take the necessary steps to make sure he opened up his office to minorities. He would no longer have a choice. It was a difficult encounter, but I had made my point.

On my way out, I looked at the security guard. He looked relieved that I was leaving. I took one more look at the office and the staff before I pulled on the large glass door to leave. I looked at the security guard and all the employees, shook my head, and opened the door. But before I left, I said to the guard, "I'll be back."

As I walked back up the street to my office, my head was filled with the conversation I had had with Mr. Krause. Did he think he had just gotten away with refusing to hire any Black Americans?

I knew this wasn't over. I knew I would have to tell Ms. Schurr about my conversation with Gene Krause before she heard it from the office grapevine. I wondered what she would do.

When I reached my office and walked through the door, Linda, the receptionist, looked up from her desk and said, "Audrey, Ms. Schurr has been asking for you."

"What does she want?" I asked.

"I don't know, she just asked where you were. I told her I thought you probably went to lunch early."

"Thanks, Linda, I'll stop in her office."

I looked around and saw Sylvia and Lois whispering about something in the reception area. Before I could pass them, they ran over to me and asked what was going on at the Fifth Avenue Office.

"Wow, Audrey," Sylvia said, "You really got them stirred up down there."

"Audrey, Ms. Schurr is waiting to see you," Ms. Schurr's assistant shouted from her desk.

"Whew, saved by the summons," I thought. I was glad I didn't have to explain things to Sylvia and Lois before I talked to Ms. Schurr. I knocked on Ms. Schurr's open door.

"Come in Audrey and sit down." the department head said.

I sat down nervously on the edge of the chair.

"Audrey, I heard some very disturbing news from the Fifth Avenue Office," Ms. Schurr said. "I heard you went down and had an altercation with the office manager, Mr. Krause, in front of his staff. Is that true, Audrey?"

I couldn't believe she was acting as if I were the one who had done something wrong. "Well, Ms. Schurr, it's true that I went to the Fifth Avenue Office, but I did not have an altercation with Gene Krause. I would call it more of a misunderstanding, and it wasn't in front of his staff. It was in his office."

"Perhaps you should explain, Audrey, and tell me just what happened. Start at the beginning."

Starting off slowly, I felt a little embarrassed although I wasn't sure why. Perhaps it was because I had done something without getting the permission of my supervisor, someone who had always been in my corner.

"Well, after I left your office, I felt frustrated and hurt. I had to meet this man face-to-face. That's when I decided to walk to the Fifth Avenue Office."

I proceeded to tell Ms. Schurr about not seeing any minority faces and about the security guard who seemed to think I was there to rob the office. I told her about Gene Krause's reaction to me and how he threw Margaret Ann Fisher's application in the trash.

I continued with my side of the event even though Ms. Schurr was watching every word that was coming out of my mouth very intently. "I know everything has a process," I continued, "and I trust you not to sweep this under the rug, but I felt I just had to do something. This was a very personal issue with me. When I confronted Gene Krause, I felt a sense of accomplishment."

When I finished, Ms. Schurr looked at me like she still didn't understand my actions. I guess I didn't really expect her to. After all, she was part of their Corporate America. I left her office feeling I had completed the first phase of my challenge. I knew there would be more to come, but getting through that first phase opened up the possibility that I could be successful.

I supposed if Jimmy Carter, a peanut farmer from Georgia, could become President of the United States and *Time Magazine* Man of the Year, I could show Gene Krause that it was time to change his way of thinking.

Back in my office, I sat in my chair, closed my eyes, leaned back, and imagined the Fifth Avenue Office filled with Black Americans. Even the security guard would be a Black American. The ringing phone snapped me back to reality. I had an applicant waiting for me in the reception area. Life as it is goes on.

*Someone's opinion of you does not have to become your reality.*

*Les Brown*

*A whole year has passed, and Mr. Krause has been allowed to keep his position as office manager while the "processing" of my complaint continues. Every time I think about this situation, my blood boils in protest. And now I get another call about Black Americans being harassed at that office. The two black employees who have their feet in the door are at risk because of harassment. I certainly can't trust the official channels to deal effectively with this. What should I do? I already rocked the boat when I confronted Mr. Krause the first time. Do I dare do it again?*

CHAPTER 4                                        1978

## OVERCOMING OBSTACLES

In 1978, the country was focused on unstable events such as the Jonestown massacre where more than 900 people drank cyanide and died at the instruction of their leader. Meanwhile, I was trying to stay focused on the positive changes in the corporate world. More Black Americans were being employed, and corporate offices were looking more and more like the communities they were serving.

More than a year had passed since I had faced Gene Krause, and the "process" was still going on. Why was it taking so long to settle one complaint? I felt I could guarantee that if Gene Krause were a Black American, he would have been fired within minutes of the incident. I wouldn't be waiting a year later for results. My stomach churned at the injustice. When was this going to end?

I had attended meetings and Mr. Krause had attended meetings. Yet, I hadn't heard if things would ever change at the Fifth Avenue Office. Mr. Krause was forced to hire Margaret Ann Fisher as a cashier, which was the first step in this process. She had been there almost a year now, and it appeared things were going pretty smoothly.

After Margaret Ann's successful hire, I kept interviewing and hiring. The lessons I learned from my interactions with Mr. Gene Krause convinced me to focus on my goal and keep pursuing my dreams of corporate success. Accomplishing the first phase of my challenge, I felt stronger—strong enough to face the tomorrows yet to come. I decided I would work hard to do my best to keep hiring as many qualified Black Americans as I could until they told me to stop. I was glad for the weekends to spend time with Nate and my children.

My days as a personnel interviewer continued to be a learning experience. Word spread around my neighborhood that I was hiring blacks. I couldn't go two blocks without someone asking me if I could get him or her a job.

Many of the applications that made their way to my desk were from my own neighborhood. If the individuals seemed to meet the entry-level qualifications, I put their applications in the stacks that would come in for an interview. I asked the other interviewers to arrange appointments for interviews with anyone I knew personally. I didn't want to be accused of favoritism. Nepotism was a natural practice for some but not necessarily for others. That standard was always made quite clear to me.

"You don't want to interview anyone you know personally," was the mantra from Sylvia just about every day, especially when she saw a Black American in the new hire orientation class. I always felt Sylvia was a little jealous that all the Black American hires weren't white. There was just something about the way she acted after she peeked into the new hire orientation classes. Sylvia was a little off-balance on the days of new hire orientation.

For my part, it felt good to be the person to give people their first breaks so they could start setting goals for their success. It felt good to be able to make a difference in others' lives.

Margaret Ann would always be a special hire in my mind. I had told her I would keep in touch with her, so I called every couple of weeks to see how things were going. One day when I called, Margaret Ann didn't sound like herself. I reflected on our conversation.

"Margaret Ann, how are you today? How are things going?"

"Things are alright I guess, but they could be better."

"Margaret Ann, what's going on?"

"Well, I thought things would be okay if I just followed the rules, came to work on time, and did my job to the best of my ability, but I guess that's not good enough."

"Margaret Ann, what happened?"

"Well, they hired a young black man, Darrell Johnson, as a file clerk, and everyone in the office thinks the two of us are dating. They are always making jokes about the two of us. They ask how we spent our weekends or lunch hours even though we go to lunch at different times. Darrell is just as uncomfortable as I am. I think they are trying to make it so uncomfortable that one or both of us will leave. I think it just might work too."

"Margaret, I am so sorry you have to go through this. I will see what I can do." That's when I knew I had to make another trip to the office where it all began. I would have to pay Mr. Krause another visit.

I decided to take my lunch hour and pay Margaret Ann a visit. It would be better this time. Mr. Krause had taken some sensitivity training, so I shouldn't go through what I went through on my first visit.

Deciding to take extra precautions this time, I cleared my visit with my supervisor. When I ran into Ms. Schurr in the cafeteria, I casually asked how the process with Mr. Krause was going. She asked me to stop in her office after lunch so we could talk about it. I finished my lunch quickly and I knocked on Ms. Schurr's open door. "Come on in, Audrey. What can I do for you?" she asked pleasantly.

"Well, Ms. Schurr, I was wondering how things are going with the Gene Krause situation?"

"Audrey, things are moving rather smoothly. We have investigated the situation and have made some recommendations."

I wondered who "we" was, but I didn't stop Ms. Schurr to ask.

"Of course, I can't divulge everything, but I will tell you what I can. First, Mr. Krause is attending a four-week program on sensitivity training. Second, we have been meeting with him regularly to discuss his views on hiring minorities. Of course, his version is slightly different from yours, but there is no denying there have never been any Black Americans in his office before Margaret Ann Fisher. Ms. Schurr hesitated, "As far as any disciplinary action that may or may not happen, that information is strictly confidential."

"Of course, that's okay," I said, "I just wondered how things are going." I tried to sound lighthearted.

"Oh," I said as I was leaving the office, "I'm going down to see Margaret Ann. She and I talk regularly, and she seemed very upset this morning when I spoke to her."

"Wait a minute," Ms. Schurr said, "What is the purpose of your visit? Can't you discuss whatever concerns Margaret Ann has over the phone? I don't want you upsetting the things we have put in place."

"I promise," I pleaded, "I will not upset anyone. Besides, if Mr. Krause is taking sensitivity training, things should go smoothly. I just don't want Margaret Ann to feel she is all alone in this."

"Alright, Audrey," Ms. Schurr warned. "Remember what I said."

"I will," I promised as I left her office.

The walk back down to the Fifth Avenue Office brought back memories. I thought about the security guard who had followed me around. I remembered the look of disgust on Gene Krause's face when I held out my hand as I introduced myself. I remembered walking into the office and seeing a slew of white faces—and not a single black one. I wondered if that same security guard was still there.

Looking up from my musings, I found myself right in front of those heavy glass doors. As I opened the door and stood in the doorway, Margaret Ann gave me a big smile. And, there he was, the same security guard approaching me again.

"Can I help you?" he snarled.

"No, I am an employee from headquarters and I can see what I need."

I walked over to Margaret Ann and asked her when she could take a break. She said she was scheduled to go in a few minutes and we could go to the break room.

I took a seat in the reception area, so that I wouldn't make Margaret Ann nervous. It was just a few minutes before Margaret Ann was standing in front of me. "We can go now. I have 15 minutes," she said.

As soon as we sat down at a table, Margaret Ann burst into tears. She looked up at me and said through sobs, "I'm sorry; I guess I've been holding all this in for so long I can't hold it any longer."

"That's alright; I know this is hard."

Margaret Ann sobbed, "It's too hard trying to break into their world. I don't think I have the strength to be a ground breaker."

"Yes, you do, Margaret Ann. Now tell me exactly what happened."

"Well, it all started when they hired Darrell Johnson. He is the new file clerk. We speak to each other and are friendly but that's all. There is nothing more to it than that. He has a girlfriend and I have a boyfriend. Every day someone asks what Darrell and I did last night, or they make a joke about what they think we did. It's so cruel. It's hard for me to concentrate on what I have to do the rest of the day."

I looked at my watch. Margaret Ann's break was almost over. I didn't want her to be late.

"Margaret Ann, let me see what I can do. It's important for you to be successful and it's important for Darrell to succeed as well. You two are the groundbreakers in the office. You have to set the example for anyone who may follow."

I knew it was time to approach Gene Krause again. I wasn't looking forward to this encounter. Margaret's break was over, and she had to get back to her station. As we came out of the break room, I spotted Mr. Krause. Should I confront him now or should I wait and talk with Ms. Schurr? I had a split second to make up my mind.

"Mr. Krause, do you have a minute?"

The security guard once again started to approach me. I put up my hand to stop him. "It's alright, Mr. Krause knows me." The security guard stopped in his tracks and waited to see what Mr. Krause was going to do.

Mr. Krause looked around to see who was talking and when he saw it was me, he said, "No." I guess he remembered our last experience.

"It's important," I continued.

"I'm busy, make an appointment."

"This will only take a few minutes. It's an employee matter that I think we can easily straighten out. When would be a good time to talk with you about this?"

"Alright, let's get this over with. Come into my office," he growled.

I guessed the sensitivity training hadn't kicked in yet.

The security guard backed away and watched from a distance.

As I walked slowly behind Mr. Krause into his office, I was remembering the last time I was there—the cold reception, the rude behavior, the unsatisfying ending.

Krause took a seat behind his desk. Since he didn't offer me a seat, I sat down in the chair across from him.

"What's this about?" he asked coldly.

"Well," I started," you have two Black American employees who are being harassed by your office staff."

"What do you mean?"

"Margaret Ann Fisher and Darrell Johnson are the office joke."

"Well, that's their fault, what do you want me to do about it?"

"No, you do not understand the problem. Margaret Ann and Darrell are not involved with each other, but your office staff teases them and harasses them every day as if they were. It's embarrassing to both of them."

"Why are you coming to me with this?" Krause asked.

"They could charge you with creating a hostile work environment."

"Me? Why me? What do I have to do with this?"

"It's your office and your staff and you are responsible for both."

"What do you want me to do?"

"Talk to your staff about respecting others and respecting diversity."

"And, if I don't?"

"If you don't and things don't change, I will be forced to report this situation to the proper authorities."

"Fine, I'll do what I can, but I can't make people like each other."

"That's not what I'm asking. I'm just asking for the harassment to stop. Maybe your staff members will find that Margaret Ann and Darrell are nice people and have feelings just as they do."

"Is there anything else?"

"No," I said, "thanks for your time." I got up to leave and repeated, "Thank you for your time."

I walked out of his office and smiled at Margaret Ann on my way out. "Everything will be alright," I whispered.

I had faced Gene Krause again and felt confident things would be better for Margaret Ann and Darrell. Most of all, I wanted Margaret Ann to see that I had not given up and that she and Darrell couldn't give up either. Tomorrow may bring another obstacle, but at least for today, it was one more obstacle we had overcome.

*Success is to be measured not so much by the position that one has reached in life as by the obstacles which he has overcome.*

*Booker T. Washington*

*Four years have passed since I was promoted to recruiter. I am proud to be in a position to help others achieve their goals, and now that opportunity is threatened. How should I respond when Ms. Schurr informs me that I am helping too many minorities achieve their goals—that referring too many qualified minorities is a problem for the organization?*

*My thoughts race, "How can hiring 3% minorities be too many? Whites are still in control of everything. They must be frightened that if there are too many of us, maybe they will lose some control. Should I speak out against this injustice or hold my tongue?"*

CHAPTER 5                                    1980

# ABILITY, BREAKS, AND COURAGE

The decade of the eighties was a time for progress as well as speaking out for what you believed in. Prince Charles went against the rules and married a kindergarten teacher named Diana. President Ronald Reagan nominated Sandra Day O'Connor as the first woman to the Supreme Court. The Voyager 2 blasted off, and the nation was amazed at the pictures sent back to earth.

Black Americans were making their mark. Michael Jordan was the NBA basketball-scoring leader. During the summer Olympics, Florence Joyner, Flo Jo, sped across the finish line, setting the world record for the 100-meter dash.

Some things, however, still hadn't changed in the black community. When white women entered the work force to embark on a career, it was seen as a positive. They were supported by other white women and identified as assertive. When black women entered the work force, they and other black women questioned whether they were taking work away from black men.

Black women were (and are) deeply concerned about the self-confidence of black men. Growing up, we were always told that the black man is the head of the household and all decisions should come through him. Although the country was changing and there were more opportunities for black women, there was still a hesitation to take those opportunities. So many young black women repressed their goals or their own career aspirations if there was even a hint of an opportunity for a black man.

Even so, my in-basket was overrun with potential candidates for open positions, and my out-basket was filled with applications that needed to be filed for future consideration. The company was growing and adding satellite offices throughout the county. My calendar was booked with scheduled interviews.

One particular morning seemed to speed by. I looked up from my desk and saw Ms. Schurr coming into my office. She sat down in the chair across from my desk. "This is unusual," I thought but said nothing.

"Good morning, Audrey. I have something I would like to discuss with you." She had a serious tone this morning. I knew she had something important to discuss.

"What is it Ms. Schurr? Are things going badly at the Fifth Avenue Office?"

"No, this has nothing to do with that."

"Oh, what is it then?"

"Audrey, you have been here four years now, and as you know, we are responsible for making sure we are in compliance with EEOC guidelines for our hiring practices. One percent of all hires are to be minorities."

"I don't think that is an issue for me, Ms. Schurr. I have certainly been hiring my share lately," I said with a smile.

"Yes, I know, Audrey, and that's the problem."

"Huh, I don't understand."

"Well, we are to hire only 1% per month. You have been tipping the scale at almost 3%."

I felt myself getting annoyed. "So, I'm 2% over the limit. What's the concern as long as they meet the minimum qualifications for the job? I'm not passing up white applicants and only looking at black applicants. I'm hiring the best-qualified person for the job, and sometimes it happens to be a minority."

Ms. Schurr was staring at me. I guess this conversation wasn't going the way she had planned.

"No matter how much progress Black Americans are making, we are never going to be done with this race thing," I said matter-of-factly. It was becoming clear that my encounter with Gene Krause was just the tip of the iceberg. This was going to be an uphill battle all the way.

I continued, "Ms. Schurr, what do you want me to do? Do you want me to tell you what color the candidate is before I make an offer? Do you want me to check the list and do the calculations before I extend an offer to any Black Americans so I don't exceed the allowable limit? What if the next candidate isn't qualified and we are over our allowable limit? Should I hire the unqualified white candidate to keep us within EEOC guidelines?"

Ms. Schurr stood up, looking disgusted. I knew I was over the line, but I was so angry I couldn't stop myself.

"Audrey, I think you are blowing things out of proportion. All I am asking is that you abide by the standards that are set for us." Ms. Schurr turned and walked out of my office. I was left sitting there, feeling alone in my world. I couldn't even believe this conversation had taken place. I looked at my watch and was glad it was almost lunchtime. I needed to get away and rethink this whole conversation, my goals, my job, and my whole career path.

I went to lunch a little early and walked to the park across the street to think things out. It was a warm day and a vendor was in the park. I walked slowly up to the vendor. "I'll have a hot dog with everything on it, a Coke, and a bag of chips." I took my lunch almost without even thinking and walked over to an empty bench. I was glad I had beaten the lunch crowd because I needed some private time to think things through.

"What do I do now?" I asked myself. "I guess I'll just take it slowly. There's no easy answer to this situation. I'll just have to be careful to make sure I hire as many white applicants as I do black applicants. I wonder if the other interviewers have to worry about how many minorities and how many whites they hire. Is it just me? Oh well, it's time to go back and face the situation. I did okay with the Gene Krause situation, I can do okay with this one too."

I got up slowly and put the rest of my lunch in the trash barrel. I didn't have much of an appetite. I had just needed a distraction. On my way back to the office, I thought about asking the other interviewers if Ms. Schurr had had this same talk with them, but I decided against it. I didn't need any more attention regarding racial issues just yet. "Maybe later," I smiled.

As I walked back into the office and down the hallway, no one seemed to be aware of anything out of the ordinary. Hopefully Ms. Schurr didn't share our conversation from this morning.

Sylvia and Lois came out of the break room together. "How was lunch, Audrey?" asked Sylvia.

"What's it like outside?" asked Lois.

"Fine," I said. "It's great outside, not too cold and not too hot, just about perfect." I thought to myself, "The weather is about the only thing that is perfect today."

Continuing down the hall to my office as if nothing were bothering me, I sat down and pulled out a pile of applications. Deciding I would make my own rules for their game, I sorted the applications into two piles. Race categories were still on applications, so it was easy to sort between white applications and black applications. I decided to call in the same number of white applicants for interviews as minority applicants. At least that was the first shot at trying to even out the scales. I wanted to keep my job. I had gotten this far and didn't want to turn back now.

I took the list of open positions and the two stacks of applications and cleared a spot on my desk. Since Ms. Schurr was inferring that I only hired black applicants, I would make sure I could account for my actions.

For each opening, I chose one white applicant and one Black American applicant. This process would slow things down, but it would help me keep within the guidelines that Ms. Schurr set. I'll bet if the federal agencies knew that I was being held to these crazy procedures, they would have something to say about it. I pondered as I was going through applications, "Should I or shouldn't I take this further?"

When I called the branch offices to refer candidates, I made sure to refer each applicant, both black and white, for interviews to the hiring manager. Most times, they agreed to interview both, and the final decision was left up to the hiring manager. At least I had done what I could do to make sure all playing fields were level.

I began tracking the hires by race, and it seemed as if black applicants were being hired much faster than white applicants. I also began tracking all my referrals on a chart and turning in a report to Ms. Schurr at the end of every month. A few months passed and I thought things were going well until one morning Ms. Schurr showed up at my office door.

"Audrey, can you step into my office for a minute?"

"Of course," I replied, wondering, "Now what?"

"Close the door, Audrey. Please have a seat." Ms. Schurr seemed to notice my apprehension. "Don't worry, Audrey," she continued, "this is good news. There is a supervisor position available in our Claims Department, and they have asked me to promote you into this opening."

My first response was, "Why? Why am I being promoted? Don't I have a say in this?"

"Of course you do, Audrey, but this is a wonderful opportunity, and it would be to your advantage to move up in the company. You will be exposed to a different segment of the business. Isn't this what you have wanted?"

Something didn't feel right. It felt like I was being manipulated, like management wanted to hide me away somewhere.

"Ms. Schurr, can you level with me? What is really behind this promotion?"

"Audrey, this is for your benefit. You have done a fine job here, but it is time for you to spread your wings and challenge yourself. You never want to close doors of opportunity."

"That all sounds good, but I still have to wonder. Can I have a day or two to think about this?"

"Of course. Let me know by the end of the week what you decide."

I slowly got up and walked back to my office, still wondering, "Why?"

The next two days were filled with deliberation and anxiety. I liked what I was doing and felt like I was helping Black Americans make their mark in the corporate world. Even so, how could I turn down a management position? I still didn't have my degree, and this could be my first step into management. If I didn't take this offer, the company might not offer me anything else.

I talked to Nate, family, and friends. Of course, everyone said I shouldn't pass up an opportunity to get into management. They reminded me that I would be in a position to make changes and help others from a different level. That made sense to me.

My best friend, Brenda, had a contrary opinion. She said, "Girl, just be careful. There's always a price, and nothing in their world is free." That made sense too. Brenda and I had known each other since high school and were going through this struggle together. She was also in an entry-level job with a small manufacturing plant but trying to work her way into a supervisor position.

Over the next couple of days, I tried to investigate the department on my own. I had talked with a girl who worked in claims and she told me she liked it there. She said the job involved lots of work but the days went by quickly. The previous supervisor was promoted to another department and there was an opening for a new supervisor. At least they weren't just making a job to get rid of me in Human Resources. I was filling a valid opening, and the last supervisor got a promotion. I felt better about the offer.

My two days were up. Today was the day. I had to give Ms. Schurr my answer. When I got to my office, Sylvia and Lois were waiting for me. "Well, what did you decide, Audrey?" blurted Lois without even saying, "Good morning."

"I don't know," I said, "I think I should give Ms. Schurr my answer first. Then I'll let you know."

"Okay, let's get to work, Lois," Sylvia said, pulling Lois from my office.

I knew my decision, but I also knew as soon as I told Sylvia and Lois, the news would be all over the company within minutes. I sat down behind my desk to gather my thoughts before I went in to see Ms. Schurr. There was no question I had to accept the promotion, even though I suspected it was just to keep me from hiring so many minorities. Management wanted to control the numbers, and they couldn't do that with me still hiring 3% minority candidates each month. Maybe my family was right. I could help make changes from a different level. It was worth a shot anyway.

I could see Ms. Schurr approaching my office out of the corner of my eye. "Good morning, Audrey," she said as she stepped into my office. "Have you made your decision yet?"

"Yes, Ms. Schurr, I have decided to accept the promotion." I thought to myself, "Maybe this is the break I need."

"That's wonderful news, Audrey. I think you made the right choice. I will contact the new manager and arrange for you to meet and discuss the job in detail."

"Thank you, Ms. Schurr."

With that, Ms. Schurr left my office with a smile on her face. I suppose she thought she had won this round.

"We'll see," I thought. "Time will tell."

*Success is that old A-B-C — Ability, Breaks, and Courage*

*Charles Luckman*

*Stuck and miserable. That's how I feel every day I go to work. It seems the job Ms. Schurr described as a promotion really was intended to get me out of the way so I'd stop hiring so many minorities. What should I do now? Should I stay in this position and just accept the unfairness? Should I let my dreams of success die? What do I owe to myself and others who will follow me in Corporate America?*

CHAPTER 6                                1981

# NEW OPPORTUNITIES FOR SUCCESS

In 1981, Black Americans were being recognized nationally. Sugar Ray Leonard was on the cover of *Sports Illustrated* as Sportsman of the Year. I was getting a little nervous because the only thing that seemed to be moving slowly forward was my career.

Each day in the Claims Department seemed worse than the last. This wasn't the dream job I had been led to believe. It was a boring job where I was hidden in an office behind a computer terminal. I spent much of my day staring at the computer screen, daydreaming about what could be. How was I going to help anyone from this job? This job certainly wasn't my way to a management position. I guess white Corporate America thought it was safer to hide me than to worry about how many Black Americans I was bringing into the company.

Six months passed, and it was time to consider leaving Tri-State in order to get back on track with my goals for success. While we can't choose the hurdles we have to overcome, I certainly could choose how to overcome this hurdle if I really wanted to succeed.

Success was all I thought about. It's all I dreamed about. I couldn't imagine anything less than success. Tri-State was a stepping-stone of a lifelong dream of success. I defined success as making a difference for me, my family, and my community as well as feeling a sense of accomplishment and enjoyment from the work I was doing.

Black Americans are taught to be selfless people. From my ancestors and from the elders in my neighborhood, I had heard a mantra, "Each one, teach one." I wanted to gain enough success in the corporate world that I could fulfill that mantra and give something back to the community. Hiring Black Americans at Tri-State had allowed me to help others gain experience and put them on the road to help others. I was able to "teach one" during my time in Human Resources. Sitting behind a desk in the Claims Department, however, was a dead end. It did not fit my definition of success.

Built during my time in Human Resources, I had new skills that I wanted to apply to a new target. I felt scared yet excited at the possibility of trying something new. My skills of interviewing, working with difficult people, and handling challenging situations might be just what my next employer was looking for.

I often reflected on what Auntie Frances told me about the characteristics of strength and tenacity I had inherited from my great-great grandmother. I was determined to use those strengths even if it meant leaving Tri-State.

The decision of whether to stay or leave Tri-State was not easy. After many hours of weighing the pros and cons, I began to think I had to quit Tri-State and look for a job that would help me reach my goals of corporate success. I was looking for a position where I was recognized as part of the management team as well as making decisions that affected the productivity and quality of the department. Success would mean greater visibility and an improved status within a department. If such a position resulted in another rung on the corporate ladder then I could once again fulfill the mantra of "Each one, teach one."

I knew that at some point I also had to go back to school and get my degree. Whenever I had broached the subject of promotion in any of my previous jobs, my supervisor had asked where I went to college, so I knew this was a necessary step along my journey of success.

I was unhappy in my current position and was making my family unhappy as well. I had been married for nine years, had an eight-year-old daughter and four-year-old son. I would come home in the evenings after a frustrating day and take my frustrations out on Nate. I was short-tempered and often in a bad mood. He would listen patiently as I rattled on about the events of the day, but I could tell Nate was getting tired of my complaining.

Nate always ended our conversations about my job saying, "You know, Audrey, I'll support you in whatever you want to do. I know it's hard to make a decision, but you need to decide what you want." Nate sounded a little sadder each time he made this statement.

For months, I knew I had to quit, but quitting without another job was risky. I knew I could always go back to secretarial work until I figured out the next step forward, but I was tired and worn out with thinking and talking about this decision. I would go to bed each night hoping I would make the right decision in the morning.

One morning, I called some temporary agencies to see what the job market was like. The agencies assured me they could keep me busy with long-term assignments if that's what I wanted. I thought about it all day in between customer calls and finally decided that I had to give my notice.

The following day, I went to work with a resignation letter tucked in my bag. When I got to work, I opened up my accounts and started calling customers. It was a slow day and I didn't have many calls to make. My supervisor walked past my desk. "Ms. O'Brien, can I speak with you for a minute?" I asked.

She stopped and said, "Sure, I'll be back in a few minutes. We can talk then."

When Ms. O'Brien came back, I followed her into her office. "Please sit down, Audrey. What can I do for you this morning?" she asked.

"Well, I would like to give my two-week resignation notice," I said as I handed her my letter.

Ms. O'Brien looked surprised. "Audrey, I didn't realize you were looking for another job."

"Yes, I explained to you when I accepted this job that I had high hopes of moving up in Tri-State. Instead, I stay hidden behind this computer and telephone, calling customers who really aren't interested in the day-to-day activity of their accounts. I have watched other account managers go to training seminars to learn new skills. I have yet to be asked to attend any training or what my long-range goals are. I have a career path outlined for myself. I have goals and a time limit. If I am going to be successful, I will have to leave Tri-State."

"I'm sorry you feel you have been overlooked," said Ms. O'Brien. "I'm sure it's just a misunderstanding," she continued.

"I don't think it's a misunderstanding, Ms. O'Brien. It's like everything else I have experienced since I have been at Tri-State. I don't fit the profile to move ahead in this company, so I think it's best that I leave."

"Again, I'm sorry it's come to this," said Ms. O'Brien, "but I understand."

Of course she didn't understand. How could she? Ms. O'Brien wasn't blocked at every turn. She was a young, blond, white female. I'm sure these characteristics helped her career path. Many of the managers at Tri-State were white, blond, and young. This was the profile for success at Tri-State.

I returned to my desk and tried to work on my accounts, but everyone around me had already heard I was leaving. My coworkers were coming to my desk wanting to know the details. I didn't want to talk about the details. I just wanted to get through the next two weeks and get my life back on track.

During the next two weeks, each day seemed longer than the last. It was finally over and everyone wished me well as I gathered up my personal belongings and said goodbye.

By the time I got home, I was exhausted yet felt rejuvenated. While I still didn't know if the decision I had made was good or bad, at least I had changed the course of my life. I had taken charge of my own destiny. Nate had not arrived home yet, and it was great to have the house to myself for at least an hour. I made a cup of tea and retired to a relaxing bubble bath. As I stepped out of the tub, I looked at the clock and realized I still had time to start dinner. When Nate and our children arrived, dinner was just about done. After dinner Nate helped me clean the kitchen. We then sat down to discuss our future. He was very supportive of my decision.

I went on a few interviews but another job offer didn't come my way. I called a temporary agency, and they told me they had a long-term secretarial job if I wanted it. I decided to take it but still promised myself to stay true to my goals.

I approached this job as a new opportunity, choosing my wardrobe as carefully as if I were an executive in this company, a nuclear energy company called Marjorang. They had just signed a new contract and were building the division to accommodate all the work that would need to be done.

Upon arriving on my first day of work, a human resource manager led me to a trailer which was located in a large lot adjacent to the main building. The trailer had been converted into an office. I guess my expression gave away my surprise because the manager quickly told me permanent offices were being arranged at the main building. For now, there were at least 12 trailers lined up side by side. They looked like large beige boxes lined up to be shipped out somewhere. All kinds of technicians were running around wearing waist belts with tools in them.

I was introduced to my boss, Mr. Blair, a short man with a British accent who dressed impeccably and greeted me with a big smile. Mr. Blair explained that I was the first secretary hired and would be required to set procedures in place for the future secretaries yet to come on board. I was excited by the challenge but a little nervous about the expectations. We walked through the trailer that was buzzing with engineers as Mr. Blair introduced me to the rest of the staff. He showed me to my desk, the supply cabinet, and the rest rooms.

At first, the job seemed overwhelming, but I just took one situation at a time and the rest seemed to fall into place. Everyone appeared to treat me with respect. I kept my guard up but thought it would be alright here. As a secretary I was not a threat to anyone who wanted to move into a management position.

It was an exciting job from the first day, and each day brought new challenges. Part of my job was to train each secretary as she was hired, explaining the filing system; daily assignments of sorting and delivering mail; answering phones; and covering each other for lunches and breaks.

Mr. Blair took time to explain things to me in great detail so I could understand the big picture. He seemed to take a personal interest in my career, asking about my previous employment and my credentials. We talked often during those first few weeks about my future career and hopes for success in Corporate America.

Although I met a lot of interesting people at Marjorang, the one thing I noticed during the first week's tour was that there were very few Black Americans in the company. In fact, I counted 3 black secretaries among a staff of 30 and no Black American engineers or managers. I hoped this would change with this new project. I knew Marjorang was hiring because the company was growing and expanding fast.

Months passed, and I got more and more comfortable in this temporary job. I found myself sending out fewer and fewer resumes. Time was getting away from me. It was easier to get up each morning knowing what to expect than to look for something new. It felt safe.

As more hiring took place, I was meeting the other secretaries in the company who were Black Americans.

At the end of each day I returned home excited about what happened during the day, babbling on and on to Nate and excited about what the next day would bring. Nate would softly remind me that this job was a temporary job and I shouldn't forget my ultimate goal to go to college, get my degree, and become successful in their corporate world. In response, I would feel a little guilty and send out a few resumes, secretly hoping the perfect job didn't turn up quite yet. I was learning a lot about the nuclear industry, and it was fun training new secretaries. I was put in a leadership role, and I felt empowered, like I was gaining respect and learning how to manage others.

I had been at Marjorang a little over a year when Mr. Blair called me in his office to tell me that several temporary secretarial jobs were going to become permanent. He asked me if I would consider accepting a permanent job as his secretary. I didn't respond so he continued on, telling me I would receive medical benefits, vacation benefits, and tuition reimbursement at the college of my choice. I sat there stunned and thinking, "How can I pass up such an opportunity?"

I didn't want to accept without thinking things through and talking with Nate. I thanked Mr. Blair for the opportunity and asked him if I could let him know the following day. I could detect a little disappointment in his face, but he said, "Sure, Audrey, just let me know first thing tomorrow morning." I promised I would.

Nate's reaction was a little less enthusiastic than I expected. He was glad I was offered a job with benefits, especially the tuition reimbursement, but he cautioned me not to forget my goals. We talked for hours about what I should do and finally both agreed that I should accept this permanent job and start to research colleges to get my degree.

The next morning when I reached my desk, Mr. Blair was already in his office waiting for my answer. As soon as he saw me, he buzzed me to come into his office. "Audrey, please come in. Have you made up your mind about accepting this job as a permanent job?" he asked.

"Yes, Mr. Blair, I've decided to accept and thank you for this opportunity. I will do my best."

"I know you will, Audrey," he said, "I am very satisfied with what you have accomplished so far."

That day was the beginning of a new direction in my life. Finally something to smile about.

*Success is not the result of spontaneous combustion. You must set yourself on fire.*

*Reggie Leach*

*As I started to research colleges, I talked to Mr. Blair and several of the engineers at Marjorang. They all encouraged me to go after a degree in business communications. They said business communications would be a natural move for me, given my personality and my experience at Tri-State and Marjorang.*

*With this advice in mind, I felt confident in submitting my application to Saint Marie College. When I introduced myself to the registrar for my entrance interview, however, I got an unexpected reception. Ms. Grace Ann Simmons looked directly at me and said, "Sorry, I pictured you differently." It was obvious that she had pictured me with white skin.*

*Has everyone been right about the impossibility of Black Americans making it in the white world? Is my education and career hopelessly limited? Should I persevere or should I be content to stay in my secretarial position at Marjorang?*

CHAPTER 7                                    1982

# WINNING SMALL BATTLES

Each day at Marjorang passed with new and exciting opportunities. My boss was acting as my mentor, teaching me as much as possible about the nuclear energy business as well as how to run an office. Even so, I knew it was time to make some career decisions. Mr. Blair sent me to training classes and kept encouraging me to check into college courses. He periodically asked me if I had made up my mind which college I was going to attend or if I had filled out my application yet for college. I kept telling him I was still researching colleges. Occasionally, I did call a few colleges and ask about entrance exams and registration dates, but I hadn't really committed yet.

At Marjorang, I also befriended a black secretary by the name of Jen. Employed as a full-time secretary, Jen had been with the company for a few years. She was bitter, always saying how discriminatory the company was. Jen said she had been trying to move up in the company but every time she took one step forward, she slid two steps back. I tried not to get caught up in Jen's drama because I didn't want any negative energy around me.

Jen's complaining wore me down, however, and I started to notice a few things myself. I noticed that the few minorities at Marjorang were in the mailroom, the duplication room, or in entry-level jobs. There were no minority engineers or managers. I tried to stay positive but reality said I needed to take a second look at things. Maybe I needed to get serious about my career and college.

Then in June of 1982, 700,000 demonstrators gathered in New York City's Central Park, protesting the proliferation of nuclear weapons. I realized I shouldn't put all my career hopes in the nuclear industry. Things could go either way at this point.

My research revealed that St. Marie College, a Catholic women's college, had a program where I could go to school at night and on weekends. It offered several courses highlighting successful women breaking into the business world as well as the traditional business courses. I decided this was just what I needed.

I called St. Marie and asked for information regarding their business communications program. It took only a few days for me to review the material and schedule an interview with an advisor. The receptionist set the appointment for two weeks away to give me time to get my high school records and any additional information I might need for the interview. I didn't anticipate any problems getting accepted because I had been an honor student in high school and had graduated in the top half of my class.

The next two weeks went by quickly and before I knew it, it was time for my appointment with St. Marie. I decided to drive home and catch a bus into downtown where the college was located. The bus ride was only 20 minutes, which would give me time to go over the notes I had prepared. I was going to talk about my dreams for the future and how serious I was about succeeding in the corporate world.

When I got off at my stop, I stood for a minute, just looking at the college campus on top of the hill. I was daydreaming of being the first woman in my family to enter and succeed in the white corporate world. I walked slowly up the hill, taking my time, absorbing the scenery but checking my watch to make sure I didn't fool around and end up late for the interview. I was thinking about the great doctors who had performed the first implant of a permanent artificial heart designed by Robert Jarvik. Going to college was how greatness began. Looking over the campus, I was almost overcome with emotion.

Ms. Grace Ann Simmons, the entrance advisor for the business communications program, looked up from her desk as I entered the office. She stood up.

"Can I help you with something?" she asked.

"Yes, I'm Audrey Snyder and I have an appointment with you regarding entrance into the business communications program."

Even today I can never forget the surprised look on Ms. Simmons' face when I introduced myself.

"I'm Ms. Simmons," she answered nervously. "What did you say you wanted?" she asked, seemingly agitated.

I repeated, "I'm Audrey Snyder, and I have a six o'clock appointment with you."

Ms. Simmons sat down and started frantically looking through her in-basket. She found my name on an application and pulled it out. She looked at the form, then at me, and then at the form again.

After stumbling a bit, Ms. Simmons said her revealing words, "Sorry, I pictured you differently."

Ms. Simmons motioned for me to sit down. I looked at the comfortable chair across from her desk and sat down, making sure my posture was perfect. Then Ms. Simmons said, "Don't you think you would be more comfortable in a different type of program? Have you thought about nursing? I understand your local community college has an excellent certificate program."

Wham. It felt like I had just been hit with a ton of bricks.

"No, I'm not interested in nursing. The business communications program here at Saint Marie College is directly related to my working experience," I said.

Grace Ann Simmons looked at me and answered with a smirk, "And what experience would that be?"

I explained where I worked and what I had done, but it was obvious by her expression that she didn't believe me. "You can check my records if you like," I offered.

"You can be sure I will," she said.

We could send a four-man crew on an operational mission into space in the Columbia, but I couldn't find a forward thinking admissions counselor in Ohio. What was coming next?

I ignored Ms. Simmons' remark, her tone, and her facial expressions and continued, "I have researched many programs and sought the advice of professionals. This program will help me achieve my goals."

Ms. Simmons looked directly at me with a fake smile and said, "You know this program has math and science. It's a well-known fact that Black Americans do not do well in math and science."

There it was again, double wham, that ton of bricks.

"This is the first time I have heard that. Where did you get that information?" I asked. "Look at my high school math and science grades. They are all A's. I was an honor student."

I guess the tone in my voice told Grace Ann Simmons that I was getting angry. In justification of her statement, she said, "Numerous studies verify this fact."

How could this type of thinking still exist? The country had made so much progress. Was Grace Ann Simmons asleep under a rock while the country was changing? When would it stop? When would blacks be able to take one step forward without taking two steps back? Given that Ms. Simmons was an educator, her limited view was really scary.

I was more determined than ever to get into this program. I had to prove Grace Ann Simmons wrong, and I had to see what this school was teaching others. Were they starting a whole new generation of people who still believed that Black Americans are the inferior race?

The interview continued with Grace Ann Simmons asking me obvious questions, "When did you graduate from high school? What was your best subject? What was your least favorite subject? How much time did you spend each evening on homework?"

Why wasn't she typing this information into a database? Why was she asking me obvious questions? Maybe I had selected the wrong college for my mission.

Ms. Simmons had my transcripts and my resume with the answers to all these obvious questions, but I continued to answer her mindless inquiries. When she saw she couldn't dissuade me from my goal, she agreed to put my name on the entrance list but with the stipulation that I was on probationary status until she reviewed my math and science grades. I knew I could challenge her to see if this was standard practice for all or just black students, but I didn't. I decided I would get in, excel, graduate, and then prove Ms. Simmons wrong. This wasn't the time for the challenge. I knew there would be battles ahead and I had to choose carefully which ones were worth the challenge.

I was angry and yet excited, but I couldn't let Ms. Simmons see either. I wanted her to see confidence, not anger or excitement. I wanted her to see there was no doubt in my mind that I would pass all her tests and graduate with honors.

Ms. Simmons stood up to let me know the interview was over. I stood up, "Thank you for your time," I said.

"You will receive your acceptance letter with instructions for orientation within the next two weeks," she said, without acknowledging my thank-you.

When I was safely out of the building, I jumped up and down screaming, "Yes, yes. I made the list!" When I got to the bus stop, the bus was just about to pull out. My friend, Jennifer, saw me and asked the driver to wait. Jen liked to come to town from work to shop, but I was still surprised to see her. I hurriedly took a seat next to her.

"Jen, you'll never guess what just happened." Without waiting for an answer, I said, "I've been accepted at Saint Marie College!"

Jen looked surprised and said, "How did that happen? They almost never let blacks in that college."

Jen didn't want to sound mean or negative, but she didn't trust too many white folks. She said white folks always have their own agenda. Jen had been passed up for several promotions, watching a white candidate with less experience and less education get the job. She had faced rejection from professional organizations as soon as they saw she was black, so her skepticism was warranted.

I began to tell Jen all about the interview and the remark Ms. Simmons made about blacks being poor in math and science.

Jen said, "I told you Audrey, it's almost useless to try and make it in their corporate world."

"I don't care; it's going to be different for me. I'm going to succeed," I protested. I got up because the bus was approaching my stop.

"Well, good luck, Audrey. You know I'm there for you, Girl," Jen yelled as I got off the bus. I knew Jen meant it and I knew I could count on her. I also knew if things got rough, she would be there encouraging me to keep going, not to give up.

Every day after work I ran home to check the mailbox for my acceptance letter. Finally after a week, it came. I took the letter out of the box and just stared at it for a few minutes, almost afraid to open it. I went into the house and climbed the stairs, still holding the sealed letter, and sat down at my window seat that overlooked my peaceful neighborhood.

Slowly, I opened the letter. There it was in black and white. "Mrs. Audrey Snyder, you have been accepted into Saint Marie College in Business Communications. Registration hours are 6 p.m. to 9 p.m. Monday through Friday this week and continuing through next week."

I read and reread the letter, making sure I wouldn't forget a word. When I had read the letter for the last time, I put it to my chest, closed my eyes, and said a little prayer, thanking God for this opportunity. I promised I would not squander this chance. All Black Americans who are given a chance have to succeed because if they mess up, there will definitely not be another chance for a very long time. The penalty for failure is severe for all. I promised to make God, my family, and my friends proud of me.

I went to bed that night knowing I had overcome one more obstacle. I had to prove Ms. Simmons and people like her wrong about the life of Black Americans and our academic abilities. I was beginning an uphill battle, and the only way to win a battle is to win small scrimmages one at time. I was a patient person with time on my side.

*To climb steep hills requires a slow pace at first.*

*William Shakespeare*

*In 1983, Chicago elected its first black mayor, Harold Washington. Vanessa Williams became the first Black American to be crowned Ms. America. I wondered if Saint Marie would celebrate the first federal Martin Luther King Jr. holiday.*

*I wondered if the obvious racist behavior I encountered from Ms. Simmons would be hidden in the classroom. I hoped the focus would be on education, not myths and folklore.*

*I would get my answer through my first instructor, Ms. McCullough, who seemed to be cut from the same cloth as Grace Ann Simmons. It seemed the affirmative action programs that were to make sure Black Americans were given fair opportunities hadn't yet penetrated this educational institution. Even so, I had been admitted to the program. I made a commitment to myself to overcome any and every challenge to meet my educational goal.*

# COLLEGE LIFE

The orientation at Saint Marie was hectic. It was held in a large room with pegboards on every available wall space, listing all the courses for the semester with times and days and professors. The room was packed with new students and currently enrolled students. Listening to the more senior students give advice to freshmen about what courses they should take and which professors to avoid was interesting. I got so engrossed in the conversation I almost forgot why I was there. I heard someone mention the word communications and my focus shifted back to the pegboards.

Starting off slowly and easing into college life, I registered for only one class that first semester. I didn't have to rush because I would move into the accelerated program once I got acclimated to college life. By my calculations, going through the accelerated program, it would take me four years to finish college at night.

I signed up for what I thought was a basic math course, finite math. Even though some students at orientation told me the math course was very difficult, I wanted to make this my first class. It was a deal breaker for me because I had promised myself I would prove Grace Ann Simmons wrong. This course was listed as a basic math course in the curriculum guide, but it included everything from basic addition to mortgages and amortization to calculus. I knew taking the course would put pressure on me to prove Ms. Simmons wrong about her myth that blacks were inferior in math and science, but I had to do it.

My class was every Monday evening for the next 16 weeks. I was charged up and ready to begin. I met two Black American females my first day of class, Minnie and Noreen. I introduced myself and quickly learned they had received the same speech from Grace Ann Simmons that I had.

"Can you believe she would actually tell us that we are inferior?" said Minnie.

"It's really sad that she is so out of touch. If she read any history at all, she would know that plenty of Black Americans have made their mark in both math and science," said Noreen.

"You know what we have to do," said Noreen. "We have to make a promise to ourselves that we will pass this course no matter what. Let's shake on it." Minnie, Noreen, and I put our hands together, one on top of the other, and said together, "We will pass this course no matter what."

Minnie and I were pretty good in algebra. I was good with loans and mortgages because I had worked in a bank one summer as an intern and at Tri-State I had worked with loans. Noreen was good in geometry. We exchanged phone numbers and addresses so we could keep in touch in between class sessions.

It had been a long time since I had been in a classroom. I wasn't sure what to expect. When I walked into the room the first night, it was like I was back in high school. The chairs, with writing arms, were lined up across the room, four rows deep. The room was wall-to-wall boards. Chalkboards lined the front and pegboards either side. The windows were locked shut. It was spring now, and I hoped the air conditioning worked in the summer.

I'll never forget my instructor, Ms. McCullough. She was an adjunct professor who had been with Saint Marie for ten years. She was a tall woman, with large bone structure, who could look a bit intimidating just standing there. Ms. McCullough had short dark hair and dressed conservatively. I wondered if she was a nun out of uniform.

She wore large rimmed glasses and no makeup or earrings. She had a rather deep voice as she greeted us the first night of class.

Ms. McCullough introduced herself as she handed out a syllabus for the next 16 weeks. She told us a little about her background as she looked over the class. She had been an adjunct for the past 10 years, preferring not to be affiliated with only one university. Applied finite math was the main course she taught at Saint Marie. With a math and science background, she also taught algebra, geometry, calculus, and biology from time to time.

We went through the first few chapters of the math book quickly. It wasn't too bad because it was a review of basic math. There was a little algebra and just a little introduction to geometry. I was feeling comfortable with the material.

At 7:30, Ms. McCullough told us to take a 15-minute break and be ready to resume class at 7:45. Minnie, Noreen, and I went to the junk food machine to fill up on sugar to get through the rest of the evening.

"This doesn't seem too bad," said Minnie.

"Just wait," said Noreen. "This is just the beginning. Ms. McCullough doesn't seem like she is an easy professor that likes to give out A's."

By the end of the first class, we had covered five chapters and were given our homework assignment. The three of us decided to meet in the library Sunday afternoon to review our homework. We also agreed to call each other if we got stuck on a problem before our meeting.

As soon as I got home and settled in for the night, I reviewed my notes from class. I wanted to go over everything while it was still fresh in my mind. Nate had fixed a nice dinner for me as a way to celebrate my new beginning. Of course, for Nate, making dinner was calling out for pizza. That was fine with me because I didn't have to cook. The children had eaten and were in their rooms for the night. Afterward, we ate and I told Nate all about my first night of class.

After dinner, sitting at the kitchen table with my tea, books, and calculator, I had a feeling this was the first of many evenings like this. I didn't sit too long—just long enough to drink two cups of tea and review the summary at the end of the first five chapters. Even though I was too excited to sleep, I didn't want to start my homework until the next day. I wanted to make sure I understood what we had covered before I began my homework.

The next day seemed to drag. I went through the day working and watching the clock. When my day finally ended, I rushed out the door to my car. When I got home, I quickly took off my work clothes and threw them on the bed, promising myself I'd hang them up later. I grabbed my books and calculator and headed downstairs to the kitchen table. I put the teakettle on the stove and opened my books to begin. Nate fixed dinner again (not pizza this time), so I could concentrate on my homework. We did, however, eat a lot of pizzas over the next four years.

The first couple of problems weren't too bad. When I got to the third problem, I had to call my support team. I started with Minnie because the problem involved algebra. Minnie and I talked for a few minutes and worked the problem through together. She reminded me of a formula I hadn't even thought of. "Girl," she said with that slang tone of hers, "remember when Ms. McCullough put the formula on the board after our break?"

"Yeah," I said.

"Well," Minnie continued, "This is the same problem."

"Oh," I said, "thanks, Minnie. The formula had completely slipped my mind." When I hung up from Minnie, I felt pretty good. I thought, "This is going to be okay." I went through the rest of the homework with few problems.

Before I knew it, Monday evening was here again. I was anxious to turn in my homework because I was proud of what I had accomplished already. We went over the homework as soon as class started. My hard work had paid off; my answers were all correct. I was glad we reviewed the homework first so I could focus on the evening lesson. Minnie, Noreen, and I gave each other a quick glance and a smile. We had gotten through the first week.

The course was challenging and at times seemed overwhelming. We had to take one night at a time. We talked to each other often throughout each week and continued to meet on Sundays at the library to review our homework before Monday's class. Noreen had even solicited the help of one of the engineers she worked with to consult on a couple of problems. We took advantage of every resource we could. We hired a tutor and asked other students for help.

In class it was obvious to us and to others that Ms. McCullough had singled out Minnie, Noreen, and me to answer questions that she assumed we wouldn't know the answers to. Sometimes she was right in her assumptions, and other times, one of us would surprise her with the correct answer. Her prejudice was so noticeable that on more than one occasion someone at break would remark about how much Ms. McCullough picked on us. It was obvious that our math instructor didn't have any more faith in our ability to achieve success than Grace Ann Simmons did.

One evening we were going over our homework as usual and Ms. McCullough called on Minnie to answer a question. When Minnie gave her the answer, Ms. McCullough said, "Minnie, how in the world did you come up with an answer like that?" She laughed a little as she said it and so did a few other classmates.

Minnie was embarrassed because we had worked hard on our homework and worked with a tutor to make sure we had the correct answer. Minnie looked at both Noreen and me and shrugged her shoulders. She proceeded to describe how she came up with the answer but Ms. McCullough said, "I'm not sure why you thought that was the correct answer but that's wrong."

I was busy looking through my notes and in the textbook while this discussion was going on. I couldn't see where Minnie had made a mistake. I raised my hand right in the middle of the discussion. "Ms. McCullough, could you please show us how you arrived at your answer?" I asked.

Looking annoyed, Ms. McCullough went to the chalkboard to write the problem for the rest of the class to see. Half way through her explanation, she stopped. She picked up the homework assignment to look at the problem again and quickly turned to a page in the textbook. She looked at Minnie and said, "Minnie, your answer is correct." An apology would have been nice, but I'm sure this whole situation didn't endear us to Ms. McCullough. She would probably just pick on us more than ever.

Ms. McCullough quickly moved on to the next problem, not dwelling on the fact that she had made a mistake. She didn't call on us the rest of the evening. Although Ms. McCullough was aloof with the three of us over the next couple of weeks, she didn't single us out anymore.

Near the halfway point in the course, we needed a strategy to get through midterms. We decided to meet at Minnie's house after work since it was centrally located to both Noreen and me. The house would be quiet because Minnie lived alone. We studied almost all weekend at Minnie's where she had a large pot of coffee waiting when we arrived. Noreen brought her double layer fudge brownies that would become our staple during our study sessions. I brought chips and pretzels to munch on.

Nate and the children understood my time away. As I look back on this now, it was a lot to ask of the family, but we have all benefited from my experience.

Minnie, Noreen, and I studied all of our quizzes and reviewed homework assignments. When the evening of the midterms came, we felt confident we had prepared enough. Ms. McCullough gave us half the class time to complete the mid-term. She gave us an extended break so she could check the exam. When we returned, she gave us our results. The study time proved to be worth every minute because we all passed the midterm with A-minuses or B-pluses. It was difficult but at least now we could take a breath and see light at the end of the tunnel.

It was probably my imagination, but it seemed to me that our instructor actually looked a little disappointed when she handed us our grades. This was my first college class since I had been out of school for many years and I got an A- on the midterm. Minnie and Noreen both got a B+. The three of us took a vow to work even harder the second half of the course. We would increase our study time and intensity.

*The man who has confidence in himself gains the confidence of others.*

*Hasidic saying*

*After getting a final B+ in applied finite math, things were definitely looking up. I felt brave enough to take on my next challenge, a religious course. Since Saint Marie was a Catholic college, everyone was required to take six credits of religion. I figured it would be an interesting journey for both the nun teaching the course and for me to see how my Baptist background would fit into a Catholic women's college.*

*In retrospect, I should have been more worried than excited about this. For all my experience with racial prejudice, perhaps I should have been prepared for religious prejudice. Unfortunately, I was not.*

# RESPONSIBILITY TO TRY

I laugh now when I think back to the first day of my religion class. I walked into a large room that was sparsely decorated. Some of the classrooms had colorful maps or posters on the wall. Some even had nice paintings or murals. This room, number 313, was rather dingy looking with gray walls. I don't know why that room number has stuck with me all these years. It's something about the combination of numbers that strikes me as odd for this religion class. All these years and I still don't know why. It just doesn't seem to fit.

When I walked in, some students were already seated. I started to sit down when a student sitting in the middle of the room said, "Did you seat yourself according to the chart?"

Baffled, I asked, "What?"

She repeated herself, pointing to the wall. "Did you seat yourself according to the chart on the wall?"

"No," I answered, looking at the wall.

The seating chart on the wall was in the shape of a cross. It was labeled: Catholics in front, Baptists on the left, born again/saved Christians on the right, and atheists in the back. I paused and looked around the room where a handful of students were already seated. The rest of the students came in, looked at the wall, and seated themselves accordingly. I learned later that many of the students had already heard about Sister Mary Alice and her seating chart.

"I am really going to have my work cut out for me this semester," I thought as I took my seat on the left side of the room.

Sister Mary Alice came in and introduced herself. She was a tall woman, stocky build, with a solemn face and no makeup. She wore a black habit; that's what Catholics called their attire. Sister Mary Alice asked us to seat ourselves according to the chart on the wall. One of the atheists challenged Sister Mary Alice about her seating chart. Sister said it was just an exercise of introduction, a way to get to know us. But those of us who weren't Catholic looked around the room at each other and knew the chart was a way to see who was who. We knew we weren't getting A's from this class.

Sitting in the Baptist row, it was hard not to be defensive. I had faced discrimination every day based on the color of my skin, but I wasn't prepared to face discrimination based on my religion.

Many times throughout the semester I wanted to speak up and ask questions or give my opinion, but as I watched what some other students went through and the arguments they got into, I thought it was better to sit quietly for as long as I could.

I dreaded every Tuesday evening. I started counting down the weeks from week one until the semester would be over.

The first homework assignment was a debate question from our textbook. We were to use the Bible we purchased at the school bookstore that was required for this course. We could use our own Bible to support our views if a passage differed from the text in the Catholic Bible.

I knew it was risky to challenge Sister Mary Alice, but I did disagree with her theory from one homework assignment. At the writing of this book, I can't remember the exact question, but I certainly remember the discussion that followed.

The wording from my personal Bible differed slightly from the textbook Bible. As a result, I interpreted the text differently. We got into a heated discussion that divided the class. Predictably, those of the Catholic faith sided with Sister Mary Alice, the Baptists sided with me (on principle alone even if they didn't agree), and the non-believers and the born again Christians were split between the two groups. Everyone took a turn to state his or her view. After 20 minutes, there was still no resolution. Sister Mary Alice told us to take a break and we would continue class after the break.

During break, a few of us continued the discussion, trying to break down Sister Mary Alice's view. Even though we knew it wouldn't do any good to disagree, everyone was defensive because of the way the class started with the seating chart. A few of us agreed to talk to Sister Mary Alice about the seating chart.

After break, Susan, Lacy, and I approached Sister Mary Alice before the others returned to the room. I started, "Sister Mary Alice, can we talk to you about something?"

"Not if it's to continue on with the discussion before break," Sister Mary Alice said rather defensively.

"No, it's not. I . . . we thought of a way to break down some of the uneasiness and tension in the room and wanted to ask you about it," I said.

"Go ahead, what is it?" Sister Mary Alice replied.

"Well," Susan chimed in, "it's about the seating chart. I'm sure it worked well for your other classes in the past, but the students are very resentful and feel it is prejudicial."

Lacy interrupted, "It's making a lot of us very uncomfortable."

"Really?" asked Sister Mary Alice.

"Yes, really," said Lacy a little sarcastically.

"Well, let me think about this for a few minutes," said Sister Mary Alice. "We'll talk about it after break."

"Okay," we all agreed and took our seats.

When everyone returned to his or her assigned seat, Sister Mary Alice said, "I understand some of you are uncomfortable about the seating chart. Is this true?"

"Yeah," several students hollered out.

"Well, I don't want to make this course uncomfortable or unusually difficult for anyone. It is a sensitive challenging course without adding any more problems. Please, everyone get up, take your things, and sit anywhere you are comfortable," said Sister Mary Alice. Mostly everyone got up and moved. A few students stayed where they were.

I looked at Susan and Lacy and we gave each other a nod that at least we made an impact, even if we didn't win the argument. I knew that the damage had already been done though because Sister had already identified each student by religion. As the weeks went by, I wasn't sure which group Sister Mary Alice disliked more, the Baptists or the atheists.

Most of the assignments were interpreting different verses or chapters in the Bible, our views, and supporting statements. Most times I tried to keep peace and use the Catholic Bible for supporting statements, but whenever I felt strongly about a topic, I used my Bible and challenged Sister Mary Alice. I wasn't the only one challenging Sister. The debates continued and escalated into arguments instead of discussions. The class was becoming more divided rather than coming to an understanding about Catholic theology.

It was almost time for midterms and I, as well as others, had great concerns about receiving a fair grade on midterm tests. Susan, Lacy, and I decided to write a letter to the Dean of Students to let him know what was going on. We got together during a break to draft a letter outlining our concerns and how it all began with the seating chart. We explained the debates and discussions that had turned into arguments and divided our class.

Once the letter was complete, we signed our names and attached a blank sheet of paper for everyone else to sign. We secretly circulated the letter in class for others to sign. We knew it was a risk if Sister Mary Alice found out before the letter made it to the Dean, but we felt it was worth the risk. We knew there were others who felt the same as we did. I wasn't willing to fail this class and have Grace Ann Simmons say, "I told you so."

We got almost everyone to sign the letter and mailed it to the Dean. A few Catholics refused to sign but assured us they wouldn't tell Sister. I didn't know if they would or not but it just didn't matter anymore. I was looking at a much bigger picture of discrimination based on religion.

A week passed with no word from the Dean. It was getting closer to midterms and I was getting nervous. Then, one evening when I came home from work, there was a letter waiting for me. The Dean wanted to meet with me thirty minutes before class. That was all the letter said. "Come to my office at 5:30 Tuesday evening before class. I would like to discuss your concerns."

I read and reread the letter. There wasn't any more than that. I thought, "How am I going to wait a week?" Oh well, there wasn't any other choice. I called Susan and Lacy to see if they had gotten a letter from the Dean. They had gotten the same letter. I wondered if the Dean was going to meet with the entire class or just the three of us.

On Tuesday evening, I met Susan and Lacy at 5:15 so we could strategize. There wasn't much to talk about because the situation was pretty clear in our minds. We weren't treated fairly because we were Baptists. It was as simple as that.

The Dean started the conversation. "Thank you for bringing your concerns to my attention. Actually, I have done a little investigation on my own and have found some of your allegations to be accurate."

Of course, he wouldn't say everything we said was true, but at least he was admitting some of what we said was true.

"I do have a concern about the seating chart and will address that with Sister Mary Alice," he continued. "Please be assured that we treat all our students with respect without fear of discrimination. That is our policy. You don't have to be concerned about your grades. I will make sure they are fair and accurate," said the Dean. "Do any of you have any other concerns you would like to discuss this afternoon?" he asked.

We looked at each other and said in unison, "No."

I spoke up, "Thank you, Dean, for talking to us and taking our concerns seriously." As the Dean stood to let us know the meeting was over, we stood and started walking toward the door.

"Please feel free to come and discuss your concerns at any time you are at Saint Marie College," he said as we were walking out the door.

We quickly went to class, not wanting to be late. We didn't have time to talk about our conversation with the Dean but agreed to talk later. When we took our seats, I felt Sister Mary Alice looked at me a little strangely. Of course, it could have been my imagination but I don't think so. She probably knew it was me who went to the Dean.

That evening and the rest of the semester seemed to go by uneventfully. Sister Mary Alice continued giving us debates but they became much friendlier. All of us—Catholics, non-Catholics, and atheists—seemed to get along much better, even though there seemed to be an imaginary line drawn between Sister with the Catholics, and the rest of the class.

The midterm went smoothly. The midterm grade included the test and class discussion for the first half of the term. I got a B+, as did Lacy and Susan. Most of the Catholics got A's and A+ grades. It wasn't a surprise. The non-believers were a mix of B's and C's.

The next two and a half years went by rather uneventfully. There were ups and downs, but I made it through. Working very hard, the rest of my grades were A's and some A+'s. I graduated cum laude. I was so proud to be one of the few minorities who graduated with honors.

At graduation I sought out Grace Ann Simmons. I smiled and shook her hand. She congratulated me as she did many of the other students. She looked at me and then at my colors. I was wearing the graduation band around my neck to signify that I was a cum laude graduate. I asked Ms. Simmons if she remembered me.

She stared at me for a minute and then said, "Yes, Ms. Snyder, I remember you. Congratulations on your achievement."

I smiled and thanked her. I looked back as I was walking away. She had a strange look on her face. I was smiling so much I was almost laughing.

*The difficulty of success does not relieve one of the obligation to try.*

*President William Clinton*

*Things are changing in the white corporate world as well as in other areas, but I often question, "How does an ambitious, independent, educated, black female feel free to move about in their society?" Things are composed of their rules, their companies, and their successes.*

*No matter how difficult the journey, I'm not willing to let down the minority individuals who have struggled and achieved before me. I will have to take my cue from the women of 1992 who are beginning to change the face of the country with their successes. More women have been elected to a political office in November of 1992 than ever before. My hunger for success matches each of theirs. What steps must I take to satisfy my hunger?*

CHAPTER 10                                    1990 - 1992

## MOVING FORWARD

At the turn of the century blacks were making strides in many areas. For example, Black Americans were finally being recognized in the film industry. Spike Lee's movie, *Do the Right Thing,* aimed at the psyche of black and white viewers, was a success due to the previously untouched topics of racial situations, ethnic tensions, and anger. Spike Lee was even nominated for the best original screenplay.

Barack Obama graduated from Harvard Law School, where he was the first Black American President of the Harvard Law Review. Sharon Pratt Kelly was the first Black American woman elected as mayor of Washington, D.C. Roselyn Payne Epps became the first Black American woman president of the American Medical Association, and Debbie Turner became the third Black American Miss America.

I had been comfortable in my job at Marjorang because they seemed to accept me there. I knew that working as a secretary was far from my goals of being successful in the white corporate world, but should I make a career change now? Could I leave my comfort zone? Could I adjust to a new situation, new rules, and new people?

In the beginning I had looked forward to the opportunities I thought this job would provide. Eventually, I realized the job didn't challenge my mind or keep me focused on my goal to make it to the next step on the ladder to success. In my head I knew I needed to make the change, but in my heart, I was a little afraid of the unknown. I asked myself, "Where do I begin? How do I start over? Is it time to make a U-turn in my life so I can complete the circle?"

I went back to Saint Marie College and took advantage of their resume service, spending several hours with the resume staff. It was surprising how much I'd already accomplished in a short period of time at Marjorang. The leadership role, setting up procedures, and directing others were all good qualifications for moving toward my success. The resume team made sure all my skill sets were included in my resume.

Resume in tow, my Sunday ritual was to get up early and go to church to thank God for all that I had accomplished so far and ask that I find my dream job in the Sunday Classifieds. When I returned home from church, I sat at the kitchen table with my coffee and the Classifieds. I highlighted all the jobs related to human resources because that was the only field where I had professional experience. I had to draw from what I knew. If I could get in on the bottom floor of a company, I knew I could work my way to the top.

I spent several weeks looking through Classifieds in the local newspapers. I applied for several positions and went on several interviews, but no one was interested in hiring me. I hadn't expected getting a new job would be so hard now that I had my degree. What else? What did I need now? What more was required of me? Would I be stuck in a dead-end job and never reach my goals for success? It was the commitment to answer that question with a resounding, "NO!" that made me try even harder.

Finally, one evening after an exhausting day at work, I found a job in the Classifieds that sounded appealing. A new call center was being built. The company was looking for call center phone representatives and managers. Even though I had never worked in a call center, I thought I would apply for a manager position with my college degree. The call center was located downtown, and I had missed working downtown. I sent my resume and waited to be called for an interview.

A week after I submitted my resume for the call center manager position, I was called for an interview. By this time, I had been on enough interviews that I wasn't nervous about the process. In fact, I was looking forward to my Friday 11:00 a.m. appointment, praying for a positive outcome.

On Thursday evening, I hurried home from work and made a quick dinner so I could prepare for the next day, which I had scheduled as a vacation day. I decided to lay out my clothes so I'd have one less thing to worry about in the morning. I went to my closet to see what would be appropriate. After searching for just the right outfit, I decided on my navy blue suit.

With that decision made, I stretched out across the bed and looked over my resume so I'd be prepared for any questions about my background. I looked over the information I had been collecting from newspaper articles about the new call center. I had discovered it was a bank, First National City Bank, and I wanted to be prepared to ask the right questions about the company.

Morning came quickly. I dressed carefully, not wanting to ruin my nylons or get makeup on my clothes. My hair looked good because I had gone to the hairdresser two days before my interview. I was still wearing the pageboy although it had grown a little and was just below my neck. I looked at myself in the mirror and liked what I saw. The navy blue suit, white blouse, and blue patent leather shoes made the right outfit. It was a look white society would approve.

First National City Bank was a tall, modern building, 35 stories high with a large neon sign on top. I took the express elevator to the $33^{rd}$ floor and was ushered into my interview with Mr. Harrison.

Mr. Harrison explained the positions that were open in the call center. He then asked me to talk about my customer service experience. I paused and had to think for a minute. I explained that although I had never worked in a call center, I had experience as a personnel interviewer which required face-to-face contact. I also talked about my experience as an account manager where I talked to my customers over the phone each day.

The interview was over in about 40 minutes. Mr. Harrison told me his office would contact me within two weeks with a decision. I thought the interview went well, but I wasn't sure. I would just have to wait out the next two weeks.

That evening I fixed a nice dinner for my family, thinking the whole time about First National City Bank and wishing I would hear from Mr. Harrison before too long. I knew I had the abilities and experience to do the job. I believed I could be successful with this company, and since it was a new company, the sky was the limit.

I talked to Nate about the interview and how I felt about the answers I gave. I was hoping Nate would give me the answer I was looking for, but he just said to wait and see how things turned out. He believed if it was meant to be, I would get the job. I went to sleep thinking about my interview and what it meant for my future.

Meanwhile, my days were busy and filled with assisting new secretaries. Marjorang was still growing, and new engineers and secretaries were being hired almost daily. Even though I was enjoying my experience at Marjorang, I kept searching, sending out my resume for jobs that looked interesting. Jen kept my spirits up when I seemed a little down. "Girl, you know you will find the right job. It's just a matter of waiting it out," she would say.

The waiting was killing me. I received a few positive inquiries from my resume and agreed to several interviews. None of the job interviews were as interesting as the one with Mr. Harrison at the call center. Most of the jobs were clerical or administrative assistant positions. I couldn't understand why I couldn't get better jobs with my degree. It was like interviewers knew I was a Black American before I even got there. I wondered what gave it away. What was on my application that said I was a Black American? Was it my name, my address, where I went to school?

Each interview confirmed my suspicions. When I arrived, the receptionist would slip away to let the interviewer know I'd arrived. Almost each and every time, when the interview began, the company representative would start talking about a different job than the one I had applied for. Sometimes, when I got to the front desk, the receptionist would look at me and say in her most polite tone, "I am sorry but that job has already been filled." I knew that wasn't true, but what could I do? I couldn't prove discrimination.

I would leave from these interviews dejected and cry on Jen's shoulder. She would try to convince me to just stay where I was and try to work my way up.

Jen had accepted that her fate was already sealed. She had accepted that she would always work at entry-level jobs. I couldn't accept that. I wanted more. I had worked hard and I deserved more. I was determined to have more. There was no way I was going to just settle. It might take a while but I knew I would realize my dream.

One thing was certain, I was not going to just sit around and wait. There must be something available for me at Marjorang. Maybe I could work my way up to a management position.

I requested an appointment with the Human Resources Manager, Ms. Samuels, to talk about moving up in the company. Ms. Samuels agreed to see me on my lunch hour.

I was glad I had continued to dress in business attire. In a seminar I had attended, the lecturer had said we should always dress for the job we want and not the one we have. I tried to always dress for my successful transition into their corporate world.

When I arrived at Ms. Samuels office, resume in tow, she smiled and invited me to sit down. "What can I do for you, Audrey?" Ms. Samuels asked.

"Well, Ms. Samuels, I have my degree in business communications and would like to know what opportunities exist in the company for me."

"I would need to look at your resume, Audrey, before I could offer any suggestions," said Ms. Samuels. She actually looked relieved that she could put off telling me nothing was available for me.

"That's not a problem," I answered. "I have it right here." I opened the folder on my lap and handed her a copy. Ms. Samuels looked a little stunned but started to look over my resume.

"Well, Audrey, you have a pretty good job right now," she said without looking up at me. "What else would you be looking for?"

"Well, that's what I thought you could help me with. I don't know what kinds of jobs are available in management," I said.

"Management," she said a little sarcastically. "You are just a secretary right now."

"I'm a secretary with a degree in business communications," I interjected.

She hesitated for a few seconds. "I guess you could move up to supervisor if a position becomes available," she said.

"I was hoping for a little more than that. What other positions would I qualify for?" I continued. "Is there anything open in training or human resources?"

By the way Ms. Samuels looked at me, you would have thought I had asked for her firstborn. "Audrey, I will be happy to check all available openings and get back in touch with you."

I could tell by the expression on her face that this would be the last time I spoke with Ms. Samuels about openings. I stood up to let Ms. Samuels know I was through with this interview. "Thanks for your time, Ms. Samuels," I said as I offered my hand to her.

She too knew that this was the last time we would talk. She said, "Good luck, Audrey," as she shook my hand.

I had my answer. I had to look outside Marjorang if I was going to succeed in their corporate world.

I still had a few minutes before I had to return to my desk, so I decided to take a walk outside to clear my head. As I walked through the revolving doors to the outside, I felt like I wasn't even in my own body. What had just happened? More disappointment, more rejection, more prejudice. Maybe Jen was right. Maybe my fate was already sealed.

I returned to my desk after walking around the building a couple of times. I thought about Ms. Samuel's offer of a supervisor. The more I thought about it, the angrier I got. I tried to work but couldn't focus. After about 30 minutes, I went to Mr. Blair and told him all about my interview with Ms. Samuels. I asked Mr. Blair if I could go home for the rest of the afternoon because I was getting a terrible headache.

He said, "Of course." While Mr. Blair understood, it almost seemed unfair that I was interviewing to leave him. He even said that if I wasn't able to come in the next day and needed another day to just give him a call in the morning. I thanked him but told him I was sure I would be able to return the following day. I wondered how many more tomorrows I could keep coming back to this same job with no future for success. Could I keep coming back?

I walked out the door feeling lower and more depressed than I had in a long time. I got in my car, rolled down the window, and just stared out into the parking lot. Nothing seemed important at this point. I knew life came with disappointments and failures that I had to adjust to. I just needed some time to put everything in perspective. What had I accomplished while at Marjorang? Had I made any inroads for others to follow? What should the next step be?

*You have to have confidence in your ability, and then be tough enough to follow through.*

Rosalynn Carter

*When I told Jen about the events with Ms. Samuels, she sat there shaking her head. "I told you, Audrey, they aren't going to let you succeed. You better figure out how you can be comfortable just knowing your place in this world."*

*I answered, "I can't, Jen. I can't be content and I will never be comfortable knowing I deserve more. That may be fine for some people, but it won't work for me."*

*Still, with a world filled with people like Ms. Samuels and mysteriously "filled" jobs, how am I going to get the job I know I deserve? What is the next right step?*

## OPPORTUNITY KNOCKS

It had been a long week filled with anxiety, disappointment, and anger. I was glad when Friday finally came. The more I thought about my current position, the more I felt convinced I had to do something to make a change. Ms. Samuels only made my resolve stronger.

After a quick breakfast, I hurried to my car, picking up the morning paper in the driveway on my way out. I checked the mailbox because I had forgotten to check it when I came home the night before. I put the few pieces of mail in my bag with my resume and lunch.

Jen, who shared driving responsibilities with me, was waiting on the corner. I tried not to argue with Jen about her negative feelings about advancement. We were never going to agree on the struggle, and I didn't want to fill my days with negative feelings.

I walked from the parking lot to the main entrance of Marjorang, thinking about the job interviews I had been on. I kept thinking about the call center at First National City Bank and wondering when I would hear from them. When I got to my desk, I opened my bag and started going through the mail I had grabbed from my mailbox. There were advertisements, the phone bill, and then a letter with a return address I didn't recognize.

I opened the letter quickly. It was from First National and went as follows:

> Dear Ms. Snyder,
>
> We have been reviewing the applications of all the candidates that interviewed for the position of Customer

Service Representative. You have been selected as a successful candidate and we would like to discuss an offer with you.

Please contact us at the phone number listed below at your earliest convenience.

Sincerely,


Walter Harrison
First National City Bank


"Wow," I hollered without even thinking. Everyone around me looked up. "I'm sorry, I just read some very exciting news," I said. I knew I was beaming, smiling from ear to ear.

I left my desk and went to the pay phones in the hall. "That's great, Audrey," Jen yelled back in the phone. "I know how much you want this job, and I'm so happy for you."

The morning went quickly, and finally it was lunch hour, my opportunity to call Mr. Harrison. I grabbed my purse and hurried to the pay phones in the hall. I dialed the number and a woman answered, "Good afternoon, First National City Bank, how can I help you?"

"Good afternoon," I answered back. "I would like to speak to Mr. Walter Harrison."

"One moment, I'll connect you."

"Good afternoon, Mr. Harrison's office," said a voice on the other end.

"Good afternoon, this is Audrey Snyder. I received a letter from Mr. Harrison about a job at the call center."

"Yes, Ms. Snyder, I have Mr. Harrison's calendar. When can you come in?" the voice asked.

"I can come tomorrow on my lunch hour if that's okay," I said, trying not to sound too excited.

"That should be fine. I'll put you in for noon tomorrow," the voice answered back.

That didn't take very long. I still had half of my lunch hour left. I decided to shop on my lunch hour because I was too excited to eat. Hecht's department store in a nearby strip mall always had good sales. I wanted to look at jewelry. Maybe I would buy a nice pin and some new earrings for tomorrow's appointment.

I threw my sandwich away and headed to Hecht's. It was a large department store with a jewelry department on the first floor. Walking over, I thought about what I should wear the following day. For my first interview at First National I had worn my navy blue suit, so I decided to wear my beige suit with my yellow blouse for this appointment.

Walking around the jewelry counter at Hecht's was one of my favorite things to do on my lunch hour. The red clearance signs caught my eye, and I headed in that direction. There were tables and tables of gold jewelry. I took my time. I didn't have to buy anything, but if I saw something nice that would make my suit a little more special, I would get it.

I was just about to leave when I noticed a gold pin in the shape of a four-leaf clover. "How appropriate," I thought, "a lucky charm." I wondered if I could find earrings to match.

I spun the rack around and there they were. I quickly grabbed the pin and earrings and took them to the checkout counter. Feeling great about my purchase, I headed back to work with my bag tucked under my arm and a big smile on my face.

*If opportunity doesn't knock, build a door.*

*Milton Berle*

*Today is the day that can change the direction of my career. It can be a new beginning for me, the first step on that ladder for success.*

*It is my turn now. I can feel it. I have been preparing for this day for as long as I can remember. As with the women and minorities who are taking roles in President William Clinton's cabinet, it is time for me to take on a bigger, more important role.*

*A little scared of the challenges ahead, I still feel ready for Mr. Harrison and any offer he might make today. Of course, I don't anticipate the wrinkle that is coming.*

# BREAKING DOWN DOORS

When I reached the First National City Bank complex, I hesitated before entering. I stood outside of the building and said a prayer, asking God to make this my opportunity. I thanked God for this chance and went inside to greet the receptionist. She was ready for me. "Good afternoon, Ms. Snyder. Mr. Harrison is waiting for you."

"Thank you," I said and followed her into Mr. Harrison's office.

"Please have a seat, Ms. Snyder," Mr. Harrison said. He was dressed in a gray pinstriped suit, light blue shirt, and a blue and gray print tie. He looked so professional. I couldn't help but think this company was on the right track.

"Thank you," I said as I sat down.

Mr. Harrison started, "We are glad you are interested in First National City Bank, Ms. Snyder. We are prepared to offer you a position as a customer service representative with a starting salary of $22,000."

The expression on my face must have given away the shock at the low salary because he continued. "That is $2,000 more than we are offering everyone else. We are taking into consideration that you have a degree and experience with customers. There are many opportunities to move into different positions as we build this call center," he continued, but I didn't hear much after $22,000. I had expected so much more as I was already making $30,000. I was prepared for a small cut but not a $7,000 a year cut.

I sat numb for a few minutes but knew I needed to regroup if I wanted to be an employee of First National. "Thank you for the offer,

Mr. Harrison. Can you tell me a little about the benefits of working for First National City Bank?" I asked, trying to smile a little.

"Sure," he continued. "The health benefits are paid by First National. You will have medical, dental, and vision benefits. And there is tuition refund if you wish to continue on with your education. Here is some detailed information regarding our benefit package," he said as he handed me a folder of papers.

I was still trying to take all of this in and felt pressure to give a decision right there on the spot. I was trying to add the advantage of medical coverage onto $22,000. Even though I was making $30,000 at Marjorang, I was paying a portion of my medical benefits. I could go for my master's degree and that would make the offer a little more enticing.

"When would you want me to start?" I asked.

"The training period is four weeks long. We would like you to give two-week's notice to your current employer and start right after that."

I left Mr. Harrison's office with a lot to think about and not much time to make a decision. I needed to talk to Nate before I gave my decision to Mr. Harrison, a decision that could change my career forever. It was unnerving to think of a drastic pay cut. I would need to look at our budget and see if we could really afford to do this.

When I got home, I went in, changed my clothes, and put everything away. I sat and thought about the offer from Mr. Harrison. Nate wasn't home yet, so I decided to put all the positives and negatives on paper to compare what I would be giving up. I wrote down all the things I had already accomplished since graduating from high school and college, and in my positions at Tri-State and Marjorang. I knew that sometimes you have to step back before you can move forward. I believed you sometimes have to climb over some rocks to reach the light at the end of the tunnel.

The tuition reimbursement was a big plus. I could continue my post-college education. Finances were the biggest risk that I could see in accepting the offer, and I guessed if I needed to make a sacrifice, it made more sense to do it at the beginning of my career rather than later.

Nate and the children were walking in the door as I was finishing up my list. After the children were settled for the night, Nate and I sat drinking iced tea and talking about Mr. Harrison's offer.

Nate said to weigh the options, including the payoff in the end if we make the sacrifice now. He told me not worry about the loss of income. Nate said we would work that part out. The important thing was to do what I thought was best. I told him about the benefit package and the tuition refund. The more I repeated the offer, the better it sounded.

We talked about my time away from Nate and the children and the additional responsibility he would take on. Nate said he didn't mind as long as I was happy and the job led to accomplishing my goals.

It was Auntie Frances who ultimately convinced me that I had to take this opportunity. She didn't tell me to take the job but asked what I would do if I didn't. "Are you keeping your options open?" She started asking questions, "What else is out there waiting for you? Can you financially make the sacrifice? Do you want to continue on with your education?"

I thought for a minute. "Auntie, if I can make the sacrifice, getting my master's degree will give me one more weapon to fight the struggle," I said.

"Well, that sounds like a good plan," Auntie said.

"Thanks so much, Auntie, for putting things in perspective for me. I knew you were the right person to talk to. I am going to accept this offer. I sort of knew in my heart it was the right decision and now

I know in my head. Thanks so much for always being there. I love you, Auntie."

"Good night, Audrey, sleep tight and go get your weapon!"

*If there is one door in the castle you have been told not to go through, you must.*

*Anne Lamont*

*First National City Bank has plans to hire a total of 1,000 employees in my position of Customer Service Representative (CSR). I know this means huge opportunities for advancement. I am so excited. I have my degree, skills, and experience behind me. I am determined to work hard and succeed.*

*As I get ready to begin my new job, however, the old questions are still here. Will hard work and competence be good enough? Will this company allow me to succeed?*

CHAPTER 13                                    1994

## STEPS TO THE BOARDROOM

My first day of orientation at First National City Bank was in the fall
of 1994. About 100 new financial Customer Service Representatives
(CSRs) started when I did. We were divided up into diverse groups of
20 CSRs per team. There were men, women, young, old, black, white,
Asian—quite a mix. I struck up a friendship with another black girl
named Skyler. Her name struck me as odd for a black woman, but she
said she was actually of Spanish descent. Her grandfather had chosen
the name, a family name from several generations back. Skyler's
family was educated and financially secure.

Skyler and I exchanged backgrounds and war stories. Her story
was similar to mine. She was college educated and still struggling to
break into the corporate world. Whites had all the power. To Skyler,
power meant the ability to have control over your life. Power implied
choice. Skyler was determined she would gain the power she needed
to make the choices she wanted for her future. We both had made inroads but were guarded as to whether *they* were really letting us break
through.

The morning went quickly and we were dismissed with an hour
for lunch. My team agreed to eat lunch together in the new cafeteria
so we could get to know each other. We all took turns talking about
our experiences and ourselves. We agreed to help each other through
the training period.

First National City was an established bank. They had branches
in surrounding cities and managed some business overseas. The plan
was to close down some of the call centers in neighboring cities and
manage all the accounts from Ohio. We were learning how to do this

so it would be seamless for the customer. By the end of the four-week training period, we'd be ready. I was glad we were working in teams for support even though I felt confident about what I had already learned. Of course, Skyler and I were a team within a team. We were becoming inseparable.

By the end of each day, I was tired but felt good. This was a different kind of tired. It was a fulfilling tiredness stemming from new challenges and new opportunities. Skyler and I were taking information home at night to study, and we exchanged ideas every day. The weeks went by quickly. Our team had kept its commitment to help each other. When we saw someone struggling with new information, we cut lunch short and spent the time studying with anyone who needed help.

A test at the end of the training would help determine who would be team leads. The test day, a Monday, finally arrived. The test, a combination of role-plays, written exercises, and some limited computer scenarios, took an entire morning. It would be Thursday before we knew our results. Skyler and I spent the next few days strategizing how we would run our teams once we were chosen as leads.

Finally, Mr. Harrison came in to announce who would be the 10 selected team leads. Skyler and I were both chosen. We were ecstatic. Being a team lead was an opportunity for power, choices to be made.

Mr. Harrison asked to meet individually with each team leader. My appointment was the next morning.

When I got home I told Nate and then called Jen and my auntie to tell them the good news. I was already a team lead after one month of training. They all congratulated me and told me to continue to make them proud. Jen and I talked for hours about my job, her job and what we would do to celebrate my becoming a team lead.

I went in the next morning anxious to hear what Mr. Harrison had to say. "Good morning, Audrey," Mr. Harrison said. "As you know, we are closing down the call center in Philadelphia. I would like to send you with a team of CSRs to learn the best practices. Your team will work with the supervisors there and will train our consultants here in Ohio to run the call center from here.

It may take a few months to complete this assignment. You will have to stay all week in Philadelphia and fly home on the weekends, only to fly back on Sunday. I'm sure you know it will be a sensitive situation because the employees in Philadelphia will be losing their jobs. They were offered positions here but not many accepted. I'm not sure how much help or assistance you will get. You will have to be creative as well as sensitive. What do you think, Audrey, are you up for the task?"

I listened intently, trying to take everything in. What a responsibility. What an honor. Wow!

"Yes, Mr. Harrison, I am confident I can complete the assignment to your satisfaction. When do we need to be ready to leave? What CSRs will come with me?"

"Although I would like to rotate the team," Mr. Harrison answered, "this will depend on the relationship you and your team builds in Philadelphia. We will start with those who scored the highest on the test, along with recommendations from the training staff."

"You and your team; that sounds great," I thought to myself.

*We are made up of thousands of others. Everyone who has ever done a kind deed for us, or spoken one word of encouragement to us, has entered into the makeup of our character and our thoughts, as well as our success.*

*George Matthew Adams*

*William Feather said, "Success largely seems to be a matter of hanging on after others have let go." That's how I feel now.*

*I hung on through all the situations I encountered at Tri-State and Marjorang. I made it through all the challenges at St. Marie College. Now this new opportunity at First National City Bank is a life changing moment for me. Can it really be time for corporate success to become a reality for me? Now that my dreams are within grasp, will I be satisfied? Will success mean everything I think it will?*

# A TEST OF TOLERANCE

By 1994, Colin Powell, son of a Jamaica-born Harlem merchant, had already served as National Security Advisor to President George Herbert Walker Bush. In May of that year, Nelson Mandela was inaugurated as President of South Africa, formally ending the dominance of white governments in his country. Nelson Mandela had spent 27 years in prison for trying to persuade other Black Africans to fight against apartheid in South Africa.

The accomplishments of Black Americans influenced my attitude as I began my career at First National. While I knew my environment, background, and circumstances had influenced who I was at this point in my life, I also knew I was now responsible for who I would become in the future.

My definition of success was shifting. I began to realize that the only approval that was important was my own; anyone else's was optional. I knew that at this new juncture it was time to stop looking outside myself to measure my worth. It was time to accept the responsibility for being the only person with the right to approve or disapprove of myself. I was still conscious of others' opinions, but I was learning to value myself. Had I always been empowered and hadn't known it?

Others were also starting to see me differently. Mr. Harrison was giving me an opportunity to show what I could do, a chance to put my education and experience together to prove to myself and those at First National that I was successful.

The fact that I had been chosen from among 100 others to lead a team to Philadelphia showed someone else had confidence in my abilities. I now had a right to expect certain kinds of behavior from others. I knew I had as much intrinsic worth as anyone else and was equally deserving of respect. What a difference 18 years had made. I had started this journey in 1976 and now it was 1994.

Off I went to the Philadelphia office of First National City Bank. The new self-confident me welcomed a team of 20 representatives who accompanied me to Philadelphia. I was their team leader, the example they would follow if they wanted to be promoted to lead representative or supervisor. This new self-confident me would finally have the visibility and control to influence how others saw me.

The opportunity to go to Philadelphia as a lead let me go the extra mile. I did not have a set of rules, guidelines, or regulations for learning best practices and preparing the office to shut down. It was up to me to devise the work plan. I took it one day at a time, putting into practice the skills I acquired from my communication classes at St. Marie. I made sure I articulated to my team that I expected a successful outcome. I made sure my communication to the Philadelphia staff was respectful and sensitive. After all, many of the employees were losing their jobs due to the consolidation.

This opportunity in Philadelphia also allowed me to put the organization skills I had acquired working at Marjorang to good use. Good organization skills had been essential when training new secretaries at Marjorang. These skills now enabled me to project an air of professionalism and gave me the appearance of efficiency, harmony, calmness, and maturity.

Working with the Philadelphia staff also tested my tolerance. I still faced rejection from some in authority who made snide remarks about black women having control and responsibility. I fought the urge to be bitter and resentful. I didn't want to revisit those feelings just yet, not at a time when positive things were happening for me. I couldn't let this wonderful opportunity for success turn into a regrettable disaster.

Accepting this opportunity had been my choice. It would have been easy to stay in Ohio and answer phones with the other CSRs. But I wanted to reach my goals. Without goals I could find myself hoping things would happen. I needed more than hope. I needed to take action to meet my goals. This chance would move me closer to my vision of success. This assignment meant taking a risk and going out of my comfort zone; it meant taking something on with no guarantee attached. I wanted to leave a legacy for people to remember me as an assertive, intelligent self-starter and hoped this opportunity would lead to other opportunities.

As an outcome of this assignment, I learned to trust myself to lead. Although Philadelphia put challenges in my path, I learned that success is a process that begins within. It means being willing to trust my instincts and yet be willing to accept a mistake when necessary. It means knowing that not all my hopes and dreams may be fulfilled at once, but there will certainly be opportunities to learn from experience.

After the Philadelphia assignment was over, Mr. Harrison welcomed me back home, letting me know that he had received very good reports from my trip. He had heard I was well organized, well prepared, and stayed on budget.

I talked briefly about how we spent our days in Philadelphia and then handed Mr. Harrison my report. He thanked me for the report and for doing such a good job. As I got up to leave, Mr. Harrison said, "Oh, Audrey, we may want you to do the same thing in Harrisburg."

I turned around quickly with a smile on my face and chill bumps on my arms. "I would be happy to do that, Mr. Harrison," I said. There was the affirmation of my success.

*The real contest is always between what you've done and what you're capable of doing. You measure yourself against yourself and nobody else.*

Geoffrey Gaberino

*With my success also comes the sharp awareness that I am in the minority, one of only a few Black Americans in a supervisory/leadership role. Only about 25% of the employees in the call center are Black Americans. It is always abundantly clear that whites are ultimately in charge of everything.*

*First National City wants to be seen as a community leader in the fight for equality. They want to be seen as a company aligned with federal guidelines as well as meeting community and corporate goals for diversity. They've hired a few Black Americans in management positions, giving the impression they are doing their part for equality. Should I speak out against this or allow myself to be put "on display"? Which battle is the one worth fighting: the fight against an inaccurate impression or the fight to pave the way for success for myself and those who will follow?*

# CHAPTER 15                              1995 - 1996

## DARE TO STRUGGLE—DARE TO WIN

President Clinton's effort to make his administration look like America continued to have a visible impact. He appointed the most diverse cabinet and administration in history, appointing twice as many Black Americans as any previous administration. Black Americans made up 12% of the Clinton Cabinet. The President appointed more Black Americans to federal judgeships (62 total) than were appointed during the previous 16 years combined (57 total).

Things were moving upward for me, too. I presented ideas regarding selling more products by incenting the CSRs. As a result, I was promoted to Incentive Sales Manager, reporting to Ms. Stein, who was a vice president of the call center.

I was immediately put in charge of designing an incentive sales program for the CSRs. I worked with another manager to design a program based on quality of sales as well as quantity of sales.

Yes, the responsibilities I was receiving at First National City were growing and growing. The opportunities were helping me achieve admiration and respect from my peers. I was designated as a subject matter expert within the call center.

Still, it was very clear that I was the "token" minority for the call center. Whenever a Black American came for an interview or was invited by First National City to lunch, I was always invited. I was identified as part of the management team so that potential employees would be more comfortable knowing other Black Americans were working in supervisory or management capacities. In my community, we called it the resident Negro.

I overheard Mr. Harrison say to Ms. Stein that he liked to put me up front because I had the perfect look among those people. The perfect look meant my appearance looked close to what society expected. I dressed professionally and wore my hair straightened. My grammar was correct, without slang, and my skin color was described as a butternut color, not too light and not too dark. When I heard this, all I could do was shake my head. The more things changed, the more they stayed the same.

Although I knew I was often on display, I didn't say anything because I knew it was important to know which battles to fight, and besides, sometimes being on display had its advantages. Managers from different departments would stop by to show clients the call center. I was introduced to the clients, and they were told about my successes with the Philadelphia and Harrisburg offices. Who you know can result in career moves, so when I was introduced to various clients, I always put my best foot forward.

As my career moved forward, I moved into several different jobs within First National City. After working as Incentive Sales Manager for a year, the plan was working and required minimal supervision. The CSRs were selling more products and the company was growing. More Black Americans were hired, and it was clear to all that an employee morale problem was developing within such a diverse workgroup. The newer Black American employees were dissatisfied with the makeup of the teams and the assignment of predominately-white lead customer service representatives.

I told Mr. Harrison that I thought it might be a good idea to let employees express their opinions in some workplace decisions. I suggested we form an advisory board, along with several distinctive work teams. I suggested three workgroup teams and an advisory group to oversee the workgroups.

The teams would include a reward and recognition team, an activity team, and a workplace issues team. The teams would bring all their ideas to the advisory group for input and approval. I presented a job description for Employee Satisfaction Specialist that detailed my proposed responsibilities. Mr. Harrison said he liked the idea and would present it at his senior staff meeting and get back to me.

I was happy about the possibility of being in charge of the advisory group and workplace teams. I felt confident the position would be approved, so I began mentally designing how employees would be chosen to serve on the teams. One day when I got to work, Mr. Harrison and Ms. Stein showed me a new office in which to begin my new job.

I was so happy I thought I would burst. It was all I could do to keep from hugging Mr. Harrison. I thanked him and Ms. Stein and told them I would make sure this program would be successful. Ms. Stein walked to my new office with me. She introduced me to the administrative assistant for the department, Mary Ellen, who was standing at the entrance to my office. The door was open and I walked in.

I sat down behind my desk in my black swivel chair and felt like a winner. There was even a nameplate on my desk with my name, Audrey Snyder, in big bold letters. It looked impressive and I felt wonderful. This was the first time in my career that I could actually say the words, "I am successful." I knew it and now others would know it too. An office with a door was a status symbol.

As soon as I was settled, I began to make a list of to-do items. First on the list was to draft a message to the employees about myself, the advisory board, and teams we wanted to set up. I spent most of the morning drafting, cutting, and pasting paragraphs, reading aloud to make sure it sounded right and finally printing what I thought was good.

As I started this new assignment, I was aware that minorities were judged by what other minorities achieved or didn't achieve. I was committed to making sure someone could follow in my steps. I appreciated what others before me had done to make it possible for me to even be in this position, and I wanted to make sure I did the same for those who followed.

My confidence level was up, and I felt like I was making inroads on the path of achieving a successful career. Over the previous two years, I had successfully transformed two markets, Philadelphia and Harrisburg. I had developed an incentive plan and now I was in an office and in charge of an advisory group with three teams—a lot of accomplishments in a short period of time. I had overcome externally perceived barriers with my education and experience. I had overcome my internal barriers with confidence and creativity. I was using my assets to prove myself as a leader.

As the teams developed and workplace issues dwindled, I was presented with another promotion and the title of Banking Officer at my yearly performance review. I felt as if I could relax just a little and focus on success instead of the constant focus on struggle. I knew I had to be twice as good as whites, but that was a given, that was a way of life for Black Americans. My dreams were coming true, and in order to get through the glass ceiling, I decided I needed more ammunition, another strategy.

It was time to go back to school and get my master's degree. I had achieved so much already that I wondered how much more would be possible with more education. I could go to school and be reimbursed for my degree as long as my studies were related to my current job. I decided to go back to Saint Marie because of the accelerated program. I could go to school on the weekends and earn my master's degree quickly.

As I contemplated returning to Saint Marie, I took a deep breath, sat back in my chair, and wondered how I would feel walking back through those doors. Would I run into Grace Ann Simmons? Would she have changed her views regarding Black Americans? Would she welcome me and wish me luck this time? As I looked at the curriculum for Saint Marie on the internet, the old feelings of resentment and fear drifted back into my thoughts.

I knew I couldn't stay in this awful mental place. I had to quickly rid myself of these thoughts, reminding myself of how far I had come. I was academically qualified to be a manager at a major bank and was appointed a banking officer. I had to remind myself of what I had accomplished using creativity, education, and experience. I had developed my own job descriptions and obtained my positions through negotiations.

Choosing to believe I had reached some of my goals, I had to make a choice to leave the bitterness behind if I was going to continue moving forward. There was no room for bitterness in my definition of success.

I also realized that reaching my goal was a progressive movement, a process. Success doesn't come by reaching perfection right out of the gate. Success requires smaller victories along the way, allowing time to reach the ultimate goal of breaking through the glass ceiling.

As I completed my application online, I hoped Saint Marie had been forced to move with the changing country. According to national research studies, the number of Black Americans awarded university degrees had increased by 40% from 1976 to 1994, compared with a nationwide increase of only 27%. It was time to face my fears and meet with Saint Marie's registrar.

*Yesterday I dared to struggle. Today I dare to win.*

*Bernadette Devlin*

As I open the doors to Saint Marie College for my entrance interview for my master's degree, I notice the inside of the building is different. Photos on the walls of past graduates display a diverse group of students. The receptionist who greets me is a young Black American female. My interview with the registrar is nothing like the one I had with Grace Simmons so many years before.

Oprah Winfrey, Black American popular talk show host, ranks third on the Forbes list of highest paid entertainers. Changing views and the success of Black Americans have paved a smoother road for my second experience at Saint Marie. Overall, society has become more accepting of diversity.

This time, administrators and teachers treat black students with respect. This time, my peers include black males as well as black females. "Wow," I say to myself, "things have really changed!"

## ASSUMING RESPONSIBILITY

Charles Darwin said, "It is not the strongest of the species that survives, nor the most intelligent that survives. It is the one that is the most adaptable to change." Working at First National City as the head of the advisory teams helped me develop problem solving and decision-making skills which helped build my credibility within the organization. Presenting changes in procedures or daily operating processes to the management team at First National City allowed me to show my skills at adaptability.

There were challenges and hurdles along the way. The most important thing I learned throughout the challenges was not to wallow in a negative place in my mind. I had to tap into my source of determination, pick myself up, dust off the wounded pride and shaken confidence, and move forward. I gained something from each experience.

I had accumulated quite a bit of experience and skill, starting with Tri-State, Marjorang, and Saint Marie College. I knew using these skills, such as tolerance, time management, positive energy, and supportive relationships, could only enhance my efforts for success. I needed to constantly remind myself of this. I had no mentor in the business world, so I had to figure this out for myself.

Each course I completed at Saint Marie benefited my job as well as my career goals. I was learning the strategies behind self-empowerment without being perceived as overpowering.

I wanted to be seen as a successful leader. It has been said, "Leaders are defined by character, capability, and collaboration." A primary focus for me was building an environment and culture where

I was appreciated and seen as capable. I had been building this culture from my first day at First National City Bank.

I realized that success is a process that never ends, with each stage having a new ascent. I knew that once you reach the top, there is yet a new peak to climb and new heights to reach for. I was up for the challenge and still wanted to find out what it is like to walk through the glass ceiling in their world. I continued at a steady pace and graduated cum laude with a Master's Degree in Professional Leadership with an emphasis in Training and Development.

A year after graduation, I was approached by a former professor, Melanie Abrams, who told me that Saint Marie had some openings for adjunct professors. Melanie explained that she was member of a committee that was looking for former students to teach as adjunct professors. I was asked to teach a course in training and development.

One day, I found myself sitting across the table from Grace Ann Simmons in a faculty meeting where staff and adjunct professors were in attendance. Grace Ann Simmons had once tried to dissuade me from getting an education at Saint Marie and now we were peers on the faculty. I was a little nervous wondering what she was thinking.

I didn't think Grace Ann Simmons would have enough humility to acknowledge that she had been wrong about me and my abilities to become successful. I was teaching in the graduate program at St. Marie, which was no small feat. My former nemesis and I were sharing information, strategies, and class notes. I had, in fact, accomplished one of my life goals. I had proven that Grace Ann Simmons was wrong about me.

*Unless a man undertakes more than he possibly can do, he will never do all that he can do.*

*Henry Drummond*

*There is a lot to think about. I have made great strides at First National City, moving from a customer service representative to a sales incentive manager, to a banking officer. I still want more.*

*Will a change in employer get me closer to breaking through that glass ceiling? What am I looking for? What will be necessary for me to feel ultimately successful? More responsibility? A different title? More money? The answers don't come easily.*

# CHAPTER 17                    1998

## THE CHALLENGE OF SUCCESS

In 1998, the first Black American female was promoted to admiral. The percentage of black high school graduates enrolling in college had increased from 48% in 1992 to 59% in 1997 and was growing. The country and President Clinton were still promoting diversity and racial parity. Poverty rates had narrowed. The black middle class was growing, so it was time for me to consider options for my future. Should I stay at First National City or start looking to venture out? Had I accomplished all I needed to at First National City? I didn't have long to think about my decision because an opportunity presented itself.

Melanie Abrams, my former professor who had approached me about teaching at Saint Marie, sent me an e-mail about a new startup company that was looking for managers and supervisors for a call center. When I replied that I would like to hear more, Melanie invited me to lunch to discuss the possibilities. She described a wireless call center looking to hire 1000 people. She said there would be at least 300 customer service representatives and 30 team leads as well as managers and supervisors, quality assurance managers, and back office staff.

Melanie said she was leaving her full-time job to work at this new call center and hoped I would consider an offer. Melanie gave me some material on the company and asked me to give her a call in a couple of days, saying she could guarantee me at least a 10% increase over what I was making. I also had the option to negotiate a signing bonus. Melanie also told me there was room for creativity, and with my Master's Degree in Professional Leadership, I might be able to carve out a nice job for myself.

When I got home, I told Nate about my conversation with Melanie. Nate listened intently and said it sounded like a good opportunity to learn something new. As usual, he agreed to support my decision, whatever I decided. I went to bed thinking more positively about changing employers and decided maybe it was time to expand my resume with different experiences. It wouldn't hurt to earn more money too. At the time, salaries were still uneven throughout the business world. The medium income for black families in 1998 was $33,255, compared to $53,356 for white families.

My interview at Wireless One lasted an hour, and I was immediately offered the position as a supervisor for the call center. My responsibility would be to lead a team of customer services representatives who talked to customers about their wireless phones. I would also have the responsibility of training new representatives. This meant I would have to learn all the technical aspects of a wireless phone. I couldn't wait to begin.

I had already made up my mind that I would accept the position if offered. The increase in salary was nice and I did negotiate a signing bonus. I had read about negotiating for the salary you wanted from an article in *Black Enterprise* and thought I would try it. It worked!

I knew Nate would be excited. I was not only advancing my career with more opportunities, but I was getting an increase in pay. Nate and I had already decided that we would save a good portion of any increase I received for our future. We would accumulate financial power to expand our ability to make choices in the future, another measure of success.

*If you are to be, you must begin by assuming responsibility. You alone are responsible for every moment of your life, for every one of your acts.*

*Antoine de Saint-Exupery*

*Even with major changes throughout the country, racism is still obvious in their corporate world. Browsing my* Black Enterprise *magazines, I keep up with the successes in the black communities. Still, there are only a few Black Americans who sit on the Board of Directors of major companies. It is still a long journey from the mailroom to the boardroom.*

*In Wesleyville, Ohio, I have friends in many of the large corporations. We all talk about how few Black Americans are employed beyond entry-level supervisory positions. Will this new job bring me closer to the boardroom? Will I do my part to advance successfully?*

# THE REAL CONTEST

In 1999, President Clinton appointed Carol Moseley Braun, a Black American female, as U.S. Ambassador to New Zealand. The *Africana Encyclopedia*, first conceived by W.E.B. DuBois, was finally published.

Even though blacks had made progress over the last 20 years, resistance to diversity, equal opportunity, and respect continued. In 1998, John Williams King, a white supremacist, was convicted of murder and sentenced to death in a case involving the dragging death of a black man.

I was committed to doing my job at Wireless One well, paving the way for more diversity and inclusivity for those who were to follow me. I was determined to fulfill the mandate I had heard in my community, "Each one, teach one."

There was no lack of Black Americans at Wireless One because the call center was set up as a welfare-to-work program in the state of Ohio. It was a very diverse group: old, young, men, and women. For me, learning all the technical aspects of a wireless phone wasn't as challenging as supervising people who had never worked before.

I wanted to make Black Americans understand that their jobs represented a real opportunity for them. They had a chance to define a career and pave the way for their children and others who were to come after them. I had high hopes for the new employees. I wanted them to rise above the stereotypes and misperceptions that lead people to have low expectations. I kept trying to encourage employees and boost their self-esteem when they seemed discouraged. At times, it seemed like I was talking to brick walls. There were challenges getting employees to report on time for work as well as getting them to understand the rules around lunch hours and break times.

As new supervisors, my peers and I knew we were being watched. We needed to prove we were worth the money and training we received. For many of the Black American supervisors at Wireless One, this job was their first chance to have an opportunity to manage at this level.

All the supervisors decided to meet and put together a formalized set of ground rules for the call center. We included lunch and break times, quality and quantity of calls, absence and tardy rules, and promotional opportunities. We communicated the ground rules to all employees in small group meetings. We felt small meetings would create an atmosphere where employees would feel safe to bring up any concerns. After a few weeks, things started to improve. Our first challenge had been successfully met.

As other supervisors came on board, I took the lead to mentor them, making a personal commitment to coach them and provide advice about their professional development. As one of the first supervisors hired, I had quickly learned the ropes and felt a desire to help others as I did at Marjorang.

The call center grew from the initial 300 hires to 600, and hopes were to build out to 1000 employees. I quickly moved into a training role, where I set up a team of experienced representatives to work with new hires. I even devised a job description and gave myself the title of Transition Supervisor after getting approval from the director. Yes, things were working out nicely.

What I didn't know was that the call center was falling apart behind the scenes. We were way over budget, and the central office was working to shut down this call center that had only been open less than a year. They wanted to send the calls to their center in Houston, Texas.

When the director announced he was leaving, I thought to myself, "This isn't a good sign." And shortly after the director left, some members of the management team turned in their resignations. That's when I realized I needed to look for another job.

When I heard about a transportation company that was looking for a director for their customer service department, I quickly tweaked my resume and faxed it to Center City Transportation Company. This company, located near my home, was the main transportation company in the county, in charge of the bus and rail lines. Within a week, I was called for an interview. At a second interview, I was offered the job and accepted it. It was an increase in salary and an opportunity to direct a call center myself.

What might have been a disaster because of the unstable financial condition at Wireless One turned out to be a good experience for me. I had made positive contributions, added different experiences to my resume, and increased my salary qualifications. The experience had been worth the risk. The time had finally come for me to be in charge.

*We were born to succeed, not to fail.*

*Henry David Thoreau*

*As I face my new challenge, the world is nervously anticipating the emergence and consequences of Y2K. Meanwhile, minorities are continuing to make advances. The Citadel, a military college in South Carolina, graduated its first woman. Colonel Eileen Collins became the first female to pilot a space shuttle mission.*

*In 1999, about 77% of Black Americans 25 years old and over have completed high school or a higher level of education, and more than one in seven have earned at least a bachelor's degree. Among Black Americans, a slightly higher proportion of women than men have earned at least a bachelor's degree. I am very glad to be a part of that number.*

*According to census statistics in 1999, 24% of employed Black American women work in managerial and professional specialty occupations such as engineers, dentists, teachers, or lawyers. I am part of the 24 percent and anxious to begin working as Director, Call Center at Center City Transit. Can I finally say I am successful?*

# CHAPTER 19                    1999

## WORTH THE CLIMB

I approached my new job as director of the call center at Center City Transit as I had many other jobs in my career. I took it one step at a time, learning the transit business before I made any drastic changes in the call center itself. I wanted to make sure to develop a network of people around me who could help me succeed. I needed to make sure any risks I took were necessary to improve productivity.

Because Center City Transit was a non-profit organization, it was important to make sure I could follow the politics of the organization if I wanted to be a player in the boardroom. I was aware I needed to make sure I balanced the aspects of both masculine and feminine behavior, nurturing in balance with tough and direct.

I had hoped to find a mentor within the organization to help increase my visibility. I inquired about a formal mentoring program, but Center City Transit didn't have one at the time. I chose to celebrate what was working, and this new opportunity could certainly work for me with or without a mentor. I had long ago decided that my success would come from owning my choices.

As my first year at Center City Transit progressed, I learned how to manage a department with a previously high turnover rate by interviewing the customer service representatives and altering job descriptions. I created a few new jobs and combined duties of others into new opportunities. This allowed current employees to bid on higher-level jobs, which meant there was hope for advancement without leaving the department. This helped stabilize the department. Senior management was impressed with how I handled my first challenge of reducing turnover.

I met many Black American employees. Both males and females were in various levels of management. For the first time in a long time, I felt hope for the success of others as well as myself. I knew my strengths and felt good about my accomplishments. That comfort and knowledge gave me the courage to keep pushing on.

I wanted more visibility, and as I learned more about the company, I learned who could have an impact on my career. I asked to be included in key meetings and built a network to increase my visibility.

I volunteered to lead projects or be part of team projects. I wanted to take advantage of any opportunity that would allow me to interact with senior managers, even in hallways, elevators, or other informal environments. I showed up for coffee before meetings and used the time as an opportunity to introduce myself and meet others. Although there was no mentoring program, I began to build a network of peers that could help build my career within the company.

During the first five years with Center City Transit, I made changes that increased productivity, revised job descriptions that allowed for more growth within the department, and gave more responsibility to the customer service staff to participate in workplace decisions. Although I had not found a mentor, I was visible because of the positive results of the customer service department. My evaluations were excellent, and I was comfortable with my status in the organization.

Other opportunities for success were presenting themselves at the same time for me. Melanie, my professor from Saint Marie, came through for me again. She told me about an opportunity to work as a consultant with a Fortune 500 company. They were looking for a part-time training consultant to work with new employees, teaching diversity.

Melanie had recommended me because of the way I had handled many tough situations at Wireless One. Melanie said I showed sensitivity and the ability to handle diverse situations involving age, disability, and lesbian, gay, bisexual, and transgender (LGBT) situations.

As it turned out, the client was Tri-State, the same company where 30 years ago I had been first introduced to the harshest of biases and discrimination. I went for an interview and was hired immediately. This was a chance to make things right, a chance to prove Gene Krause and all who shared his negative attitudes toward Black Americans wrong, and a chance to show white Corporate America my journey was worth the climb.

Working as a consultant at Tri-State was self-satisfying. The classes were composed of new managers who would be responsible for managing other employees. Tri-State wanted to establish an inclusive environment and required all managers to be trained in diversity. I conducted classroom and web-ex training, addressing managers from all over the globe. I delivered training to managers from California to London.

Although I taught many management courses on delegation, coaching, mentoring, and other interpersonal skills, the most meaningful class was called *Managing a Diverse Workforce*. For this course, I could draw upon all my experiences, starting at Tri-State and working through to Center City Transit.

Teaching and talking through scenarios and situations helped me reach a new understanding of why others didn't value diversity as I did. Some didn't think it was important and some were never taught to value diversity. My job was to help participants understand that celebrating diversity would not only be beneficial to their team and the organization but to themselves personally as well.

I continued working for the Center City Transit for another seven years, with no growth in my career. I continued my part-time consulting work at Tri-State and teaching at Saint Marie as well. I had hoped for more opportunities to open up within Center City Transit, but it became clear that I was neither the right gender nor the right race. Promotions were coming to a select group: young, white males. With each promotion announcement, I thought, "Here we go again. With all the advances for equality, the more things have changed, the more they have stayed the same."

Finally, reality hit me and served as a lightning rod. A young white male who had neither the experience nor the qualifications to run a call center was given a large office, a manufactured job description, and a title. I was told I would be reporting to him. Without seriously considering me for the job, those above me in the organization told me to report to this young man and assist him in running the customer service call center. This would definitely not do. There was no way I would train someone less qualified to be my boss.

Once again, I faced a decision. I could stay and accept a stagnant career or I could make a change. I needed to weigh the decision carefully. While this situation carried echoes of past unfairness and disappointment, I had grown and changed along the way. Success no longer only meant Corporate America acknowledging my accomplishments with promotions and affirmation.

I knew that life carried many opportunities, some that were glaringly obvious ones, and some that were hidden. Perhaps this latest injustice was an opportunity to measure my accomplishments by my personal definition of success. Maybe it was time to retire, accept my successes, and say, "Well done."

I knew I could keep striving and fighting to go higher and higher in an organization. I had won the fight repeatedly in the past and knew I could win it again. But did success mean forever striving? Was there a time to leave the striving behind and be content in what I had achieved?

It was time to stop and note my achievements. The path had been slow and difficult. I started this journey in 1976 and it was now 2011. As I reflected, I started a list.

First on my list was completing my education. I not only had a bachelor's degree but also a master's degree. With both degrees, I had graduated with honors even though some administrators and teachers thought I would never graduate at all.

Next was my myriad of jobs, each with a special experience that brought me closer to my desired destination. All the obstacles I had overcome, all the steps backward that I had accepted, all the times I had proven my worthiness, and all the second guessing that had gone on throughout my journey had made me stronger. I had grown in responsibility and status, culminating in the position of director of a major call center. I had earned a place in an office of my own, like I had dreamed when belittled by Gene Krause when referring a Black American candidate for the Tri-State office so many years ago.

Looking back, I could see that the responsibility and status Corporate America had begrudgingly given me was only one piece of my success puzzle. My journey had tested my intelligence, my creativity, my tolerance, and my resolve—and I was satisfied with the result. Along the way, I had kept my family as top priority in my life.

Among the most important pieces of my personal definition of success were an inner sense of calm, resilience, and the continued commitment to make the path of future Black Americans easier by my life work and example. While some of my black friends and acquaintances grew hardened and bitter at the injustice they encountered in the workplace, I could face both today and tomorrow with a sense of optimism and peace. I never allowed anger to become dominant. This was as much an accomplishment as the position of director.

Through all of my struggles, I never gave up—I bounced back to try another day. My resilience allowed me to move forward to open doors, mentor, and pave the way for others. My resilience afforded me the opportunity to make a difference as a diversity consultant and a faculty member.

After assessing my accomplishments and considering how my definition of success had evolved, I decided I had earned the right to retire. I felt good about my accomplishments and the person I had grown to become. I could leave Center City Transit with my head held high and a sense of inner contentment. It was time for Nate and me to enjoy the fruits of our lives of work and parenting. There were grandchildren to spoil!

I decided to continue teaching at the college level because corporate positions are not the only way to positively influence those who follow us. No matter what my task, I have managed and will manage in some way to fulfill the mantra, "Each one, teach one," the ultimate definition of success for my community.

As I left Corporate America and my office behind, I asked myself: "Was it worth the climb?" The answer came fast and clear, "You bet it was!"

*The foundation stones for a balanced success are honesty, character, integrity, faith, love, and loyalty.*

*Zig Ziglar*

# EPILOGUE

According to Auntie Frances, I have followed in the footsteps of my great-great Cherokee grandmother Ringgold throughout my whole life. While the drive I inherited from her has not always been easy to live with, I am glad to have inherited Grandmother Ringgold's determination and tenacity too. I feel that I, like my great-great ancestor, took an arduous journey one day at a time, relying on my strong will to do what had to be done.

Throughout my life, Grandmother Ringgold has been a role model for me, especially because of her commitment to the children of the generation to follow—her own children and the orphans she brought from Oklahoma to Pennsylvania. Because of Grandmother Ringgold's commitment, many children—including me—had the opportunity to write their own stories. Although I've had no experience of hiding children under a tarpaulin in a covered wagon to keep them safe, I like to believe my commitment to success has paved a road for Black Americans who follow me in the corporate workplace. I like to believe I have furthered Grandmother Ringgold's legacy.

With my corporate journey behind me, I think about what my other grandmother (who raised me) and my mother (who passed away) would say about me and my story now. I trust my mother, from heaven, always believed I could accomplish what I set out to do. And I like to believe that Grandmother was ultimately glad that I proved her wrong, even if she never admitted it before her death in 1990. Black American women DO have more options than nursing or teaching.

I know Auntie Frances is proud of me. As I write, she is in her mid-90s, still living a full and encouraging life. I have a feeling all my ancestors are proud of what I have accomplished and can appreciate how I handled the struggles and pitfalls that came my way. I hope they are proud of how I took unjust situations and armed myself for success rather than anger. I made my way up the corporate ladder without sacrificing myself.

Closing this chapter of my life, I can happily say, "Well done, and yes, I am successful." I submitted my papers for retirement, excited to begin a new chapter in my life. I've come a long way but there is so much more to do. I will continue to contribute where I can and pass on my experiences and knowledge to my children and my community so they can continue to pass on the challenge to succeed. The old adage that says, "You cannot know the sweetness of success unless you have tasted the bitterness of failure," rings true for me at the end of this journey.

*Many of life's failures are people who didn't realize how close they were to success when they gave up.*

*Thomas Edison*

# ABOUT THE AUTHOR

Audrey Jane Snyder is retired after working in the corporate environment for 40+ years in the fields of human resource management and customer service. She has also been an independent consultant, specializing in on-line web based training of interpersonal skills for first line managers.

Audrey holds a MS in Professional Leadership and a BA in Business Communications. Audrey is currently an adjunct professor at DeVry University.

Audrey was born and raised in the Pittsburgh, PA area, where she lives with her husband of 41 years. She has two adult children and two grandchildren. This is her first book.

www.ingramcontent.com/pod-product-compliance
Lightning Source LLC
Chambersburg PA
CBHW060605200326
41521CB00007B/668